D1607407

URBAN SLAVERY IN THE AMERICAN SOUTH 1820-1860

URBAN SLAVERY
IN THE
AMERICAN SOUTH
1820-1860
A Quantitative History

Claudia Dale Goldin

The University of Chicago Press
Chicago and London

Claudia Dale Goldin is assistant professor of economics at Princeton University.

The University of Chicago Press, Chicago 60637
The University of Chicago Press, Ltd., London

80 79 78 77 76   987654321

Library of Congress Cataloging in Publication Data

Goldin, Claudia Dale.
    Urban slavery in the American South, 1820–1860: a quantitative history.

    Bibliography: p.
    Includes index.
    1. Slavery in the United States—Economic aspects—Southern States. 2. Southern States—Economic conditions. I. Title.
E449.G63   331.1'1734'0973   75–20887
ISBN 0–226–30104–4

To My Parents

Contents

Figures

Tables

Preface

Monographs and articles concerning American Negro slavery have been immense in number and diverse in nature. They have radically altered in form since the mid-nineteenth century, reflecting both changed racial attitudes and increased quantitative sophistication. In particular, the literature on the relationship between slavery and urbanization has shifted in focus. Whereas earlier writers attributed the paucity of cities and industry in the South to the nature of slave labor, later writers have emphasized the role of the slaveholders' society.

No longer are students of the antebellum South content to explain away its alleged industrial stagnation in terms of the slaves' inability to perform all but the most menial tasks. Instead, the debate has centered around three themes. The first is the Southern whites' fear of an increased economic and social role for slaves. Slavery and urbanization are seen to be incompatible because of the increased danger of insurrection in urban areas. The second theme is the comparative advantage of the South in the production of staple crops. Although this advantage was enunciated early in American slave literature, recent research on economies of scale in plantation agriculture has given quantitative support to it. A third theme is the role of slavery in lowering the aggregate demand for manufactured goods, thus causing the relative lack of industries and cities in the South. My aim in the following pages is to integrate the first and second themes, using a quantitative approach.

Although many who have written about slavery have briefly touched on the urban sector, a more complete discussion awaited the publication of Richard Wade's important monograph, *Slavery in the Cities* (New York: Oxford University Press, 1964). Wade's book marked a turning point in the debate over slavery, for it stressed the existence of a form of slavery quite different from the more prevalent rural bondage. The book demonstrated that the urban milieu provided a freer life for its slave inhabitants. It pointed to the many unique institutions which developed in the cities to foster the production of urban goods and services. Wade's evidence disclosed that many urban slaves lived apart from their masters and that some even hired out their own time.

But Wade claimed that these very freedoms granted to city slaves were responsible for the decline in the urban slave population which occurred between 1850 and 1860. The complex institution of slavery was, according to Wade, subject to an irreconcilable internal conflict. On the one hand, the granting of certain freedoms to slave labor was necessary for the efficient provision of urban goods and services. But these freedoms created fears of slave rebellion in the mind of urban citizenry and threatened the important social and economic distinctions between free and slave. Therefore, urban slavery collapsed from within; slavery was incompatible with the cities.

I was introduced to this fascinating area by Barbara Sosnowski, then a graduate student in history, when I was a graduate student in economics at the University of Chicago. We considered applying modern economic techniques to refining Wade's points, for, although our confidence in quantitative methods differed, we both had been convinced by Wade's logic that slavery and cities were incompatible. My initial objective was to measure the degree to which slaves were a danger in the cities, especially during the 1850s. To the extent that urban citizens feared slavery, one would expect that taxes, license fees, and jail fines for slaves would be high and, perhaps, rising over time. Public pressure could also have been a weapon. Those artisans who trained and worked with slaves might not have been patronized by those who feared slave revolts. Families owning large numbers of slaves who were granted substantial freedoms could have been ostracized by their neighbors. But my initial investigation along these lines failed to reveal any evidence of this nature. Taxes, license fees, and jail fines appeared to be relatively minor and did not increase. Public pressures seemed to be nonexistent. I became puzzled by Wade's argument.

I decided then to develop a more complete model which would rationalize all the scraps of quantitative information available on urban and rural slavery. There was data on population changes in both sectors, scanty information on population density and occupations in the cities through time, and some data on slave prices and hire rates. I wanted to see whether I could construct a model consistent with all these pieces of information and yet not based on the incompatibility argument. Having discovered that a very simple economic model which relied on few assumptions worked quite well, I wrote the initial paper on which this book rests.

The paper was submitted to fulfill a requirement in Professor Robert W. Fogel's economic history graduate course at the University of Chicago. Professor Fogel's encouragement and help on this project began then and have stopped only with the completion of this monograph. His suggestions refined and focused my argument and resulted in the basic model presented in chapter 5. But my paper was still tentative and demanded more work, including archival research. I visited the Genealogical Society of the Latter Day Saints in Salt Lake City to look at probate records and guardianship accounts for Southern counties and cities. These records turned out to have a wealth of information on hire rates and skills for urban and rural slaves. Some of the data are presented and analyzed in this book. But because my work is mainly concerned with the change in these data over time, readers are advised to consult R. W. Fogel and S. L. Engerman's *Time on the Cross: The Economics of American Negro Slavery* (Boston: Little Brown, 1974), chapter 3, for a cross-sectional analysis. I visited other archives throughout the South to collect information on city ordinances, taxes, and fines. The minutes of city councils and related items proved valuable sources of additional information. Because of Robert Fogel's encouragement, what had started as a term paper grew into a dissertation and eventually into this book.

My view of urban slavery gradually changed as I pursued my research. The model I had formulated led me to view urban slave population movements as part of a much larger picture. The city slave market was not subject merely to local influences on urban demand and supply but also to the vicissitudes of the more extensive agricultural slave market. As I collected more and more information, the workings of urban slavery became clearer. Cities and slavery were not incompatible. The cities were just subject to more dramatic shifts in slave populations due to the availability of substitute labor and to other factors which made the urban demand for slaves more elastic than that for rural areas.

But I was still troubled about the apparent contradictions between my interpretation and that of Wade. Why did it appear to him, as well as to many other scholars, that the urban environment was hostile to slavery? Archival research answered this question. The white artisans and tradesmen were an effective propaganda machine in the cities, who searched for ways to remove their black competitors from the market. But the antebellum slave was defended by his white owner, who desired to protect this valuable investment. The debates within the antebellum city halls pitted white against white, that is, artisan against slaveowner, with the slaveowner triumphing over and over again. Nevertheless, the legacy of these debates was a body of propaganda by white artisans which observers unfamiliar with underlying economic conditions have mistaken for the general attitude of Southern whites.

My travel to the archives of various cities was supported by a grant from the Council for Research in Economic History of the Economic History Association. That to Salt Lake City was supported by NSF Grants GS 27262 and 3262. I am indebted to the research staffs at the Southern Historical Collection at Chapel Hill, the Duke University Archives, the Georgia Historical Association, the South Carolina State Department of Archives and History at Columbia, the South Caroliniana Library at the University of South Carolina, the Virginia State Department of Archives and History at Richmond, the Virginia Historical Association, the Huntington Library in San Marino, California, and the Genealogical Society of the Latter Day Saints, for their assistance. The Graduate Committee of the University of Wisconsin generously provided summer research monies and computer funds, and Princeton University supported the typing of the final draft. The Rovensky Fund of the Lincoln Educational Foundation provided a stipend during my last year of graduate work, as did the Ford Foundation. As my dissertation developed, the other members of my committee, H. Gregg Lewis and Donald McCloskey, shaped it in a most constructive way. I am particularly grateful for Professor Lewis's incisive comments during the last stages of my writing. His suggestions have greatly improved the book. Stanley Engerman also aided in all aspects of preparing this book, providing bibliographic, stylistic, and analytical help. Hugh Rockoff read the final chapter drafts, refining them on both literary and conceptual levels. Two research assistants, Doug Lawrence at Wisconsin and Quentin Easter at Princeton, helped with a myriad of details. Some final touches were added by two referees.

I hope that this book will extend our understanding of slavery as a complex institution. Research is only just beginning on certain aspects of slave life, such as hiring practices, which developed to their fullest extent in the cities. But my work is not just a description and analysis of urban slavery. It is also addressed to the issue of Southern stagnation. It points to the possibility of continued bondage in the absence of political emancipation in a more urban and industrial post-1865 South. And, in the spirit of Fogel and Engerman's recent book, my work also demonstrates that urban slaves, in particular, entered the free labor force in 1865 with a considerable level of skill. The trades they had learned were the postbellum legacies of what had been very profitable investments, and this work only suggests what became of these skills.

Did any one of our people ever take a walk through the city before day-light, and see how Richmond looks before she is "up and dressed?" It is a walk which will afford any one some new ideas of city life. Go out, say at three o'clock in the morning. You will hear nothing even in the busiest streets, save the fall of your own footsteps upon the pavements. Here and there you meet with a tired watchman, walking his lonely round, but unless you speak to him, he vouchsafes no word to relieve the silence. There is nothing to be seen but sky over head and brick and stone all around you. All seems like a city of the dead, and the dusky lamp-posts appear like so many monumental pillars in memory of an extinct population. Continue your walk till the clocks strike four, and you begin to hear the rumbling of market wagons as they pour in from the country. Now go down to the markets, and you will hear the voices of hundreds, wrangling, chaffering, buying and selling, till you would imagine yourself in Babel, but for the reason that the tongues are almost all of one kind, those of colored people. The din increases, and you had better leave the markets to watch how one after one, the keepers of cheap snack houses and petty groggeries, pull down their shutters—how the baker opens shop, and by degrees the hotels exhibit signs of life in the shape of drowsy waking men, frantically opening doors and windows, sweeping down steps, or scouring door handles. The tobacco factory men are by this time astir, and you see them one after another, each with his provision-pail proceeding to his labors. Railroad people are up, the whistle screams, faces of all kinds multiply at every moment, windows are thrown open, sample goods begin to adorn the side-walks in front of grocer's shops, the milkmen become audible, and the ice-men's horn sonorous, and so by noisy degrees Richmond wakes up and shakes herself for a day's work, as if nothing had happened.

Reveille for Bondsmen
Richmond Daily Dispatch, 18 August, 1853

1 Introduction

The neglect of the urban bondsman in most slave literature until the mid-1960s is probably due to the comparatively small size of the urban slave population. In the United States, rural slaves almost always accounted for more than 90 percent of the total slave population. But an understanding of urban slavery is crucial, because the urban experience helps explain why the South was predominantly agricultural and suggests what might have happened had there been no emancipation. Urban slavery is therefore an important topic in the debate on the extent and possible causes of Southern backwardness. The hiring and living-out practices which developed in the cities to enable the profitable use of bondsmen in an urban setting are especially interesting. They demonstrate the extreme adaptability of an institution which has been characterized as inflexible and overcapitalized. In addition, many persons have mistaken the contemporary white reaction to these practices as a successful attempt to retard the growth of urban slavery. In this view, slavery's very flexibility led to its demise in urban areas, because slavery and cities were incompatible.

The present book explores the issue of compatibility in an attempt to uncover the true cause for the seemingly small number of slaves in Southern cities and for the decline in the urban slave population. Although slavery did exist in the South's urban and industrial centers, it did not appear to display the same strength there as it did in agricultural areas. Whereas the plantation slave population grew steadily from its inception until its forced demise with the close of the Civil War, its urban counterpart reached a peak in its growth sometime between 1830 and 1850 and declined during its last decade. Some cities showed a weakening in their slave populations earlier, and a few declined throughout the entire forty-year period, 1820 to 1860.[1]

Many students of the antebellum period have tried to discover the source of this decline, and their answers have been quite varied. Some have tried to find the cause within the cities themselves, while others have sought it in the profitability of slavery in rural areas. Many of the arguments will be shown to have been partially correct, but others were clearly mistaken.

Frederick Douglass, who spent much of his life as an urban slave, expressed the incompatibility view when he said that "slavery dislikes a dense population," though he qualified his statement by adding ". . . in which there is a majority of non-slaveholders."[2] John Elliott Cairnes argued that "the conduct of manufacturing industry on a great scale always brings with it the congregation in towns of large masses of workmen. The danger incident to this, where the workmen are slaves, is . . . obvious. Manufacturing industry, where slavery exists, could only be carried on at the constant risk of insurrection."[3] Cairnes, then, believed that the problems of slavery which were specific to urban areas were those of control. Charles Wesley also held that slavery encountered trouble in urban areas, not "because the slaves being Negroes were incapable of attaining the necessary skill," but because the "incompatibility between slavery and industrialism [was] inherent in the entire ante-bellum economic system."[4]

Richard C. Wade, in *Slavery in the Cities*, concluded that "wherever it touched urban conditions [slavery] was in deep trouble. . . . The cause of slavery's difficulty in the city was the nature of urban society itself," which fostered the disintegration of the master and slave relationship.[5] Wade believed that the distinction between slave and master was destroyed in the cities because the slave was allowed substantial freedom in work and social activities. Many slaves lived apart from their masters, hired out their own time, married other slaves or free blacks, and raised families of their own. They were, in Wade's words, "beyond the master's eye." But it was not just a lack of control that destroyed slavery in the cities, according to Wade. The institution of slavery underwent a fundamental change, being transformed to a worker-employer rather than a chattel-master relationship. The roots of this deeply entrenched institution were eroded by urban life, because urban life demanded certain freedoms for slaves and these freedoms in turn made slaves almost as independent as their white masters.

In his work on slave hiring, Clement Eaton reached the same conclusions. "In the towns and cities, the growing practice of obtaining the service of slave labor by hire instead of by purchase was invisibly loosening the bonds of an archaic system. . . . Plantation Negroes who were sent to the cities and towns to be hired lost much of their submissiveness and became more sophisticated in the milieu of city ways."[6]

These explanations for the apparent decline in urban slavery fail to reveal the precise economic mechanism through which the increased freedoms were translated into market behavior—though they are suggestive of that mechanism. There is no clear discussion of how practices like hiring and living out resulted in the sale of slaves from the city to the country. Without specifying such a mechanism it is difficult to explain why slavery declined in some cities but not in others and in some decades but not in others. Any theory which attempts to explain changes in the slave labor force must involve factors which affect either the demand function or the supply function for these labor services, and none of the arguments mentioned above have detailed how either was altered.†

One possible line of causation suggested in Wade's writing is that the costs of keeping slaves in the cities relative to those for the rural areas rose over time. Wade asserted that, as the urban population became denser, the costs of maintaining control of the slave population rose at a disproportionate rate. More importantly, policing, jailing, and adjudicating costs were shifted over time from the community at large to owners of slaves through

---

†To make this volume available to all levels of readers, regardless of technical competence, I have included a few explanatory footnotes, such as this one, denoted by daggers.

Economists define a demand function as that relationship between price and quantity, holding other factors constant, which gives the maximum amount consumers will purchase of a good (per unit time) at any given price. The factors being held constant along a demand function are usually prices of complementary and substitutable goods, income, and population.

A supply function is that relationship between price and quantity, holding other factors constant, which gives the maximum amount producers will supply (per unit time) at any given price. The analytical sections of this study assume that the supply of slaves was not highly sensitive to changes in price; that is, as the price of slaves rose, little could be done by slaveowners to increase the numbers of slaves or their hours of work.

the imposition of specific taxes and license fees on slaves. Translated into the language of an economist, Wade's argument implies that the demand function for urban slaves was either decreasing over time or increasing less rapidly than otherwise would have been the case.†

Cairnes and Wesley suggest increased insurrections and runaways in the cities as reasons for the rising costs of keeping slaves in urban areas. The cities contained large numbers of free blacks whose existence made it easy for slaves to escape. As escapes became more numerous, the expected value of an urban slave would decrease, and the demand for the services of such laborers would diminish, that is, move correspondingly to the left. Urban slaves could be sold to rural areas, where control was less of an issue. In addition, the problem of mass rebellions or insurrections was, according to these writers, enough to convince potential urban owners of slaves not to purchase and to persuade present owners to sell. Again, these explanations imply a lowering in the expected value of the slave's services and hence a decrease in the demand for urban slave labor.

It has also been suggested that hostility between nonslaveholding white laborers and slaves was responsible for the decline of urban slavery. However, the hostility of nonslaveholding whites would have no influence on the effective demand for slaves unless they could somehow reduce the net income which slaveholders reaped from their bondsmen. This could have been accomplished, for example, if protests by white laborers disrupted the production processes of slaveowners. One well-known case of such disruption was the severe beating Frederick Douglass received at the

---

†Demand functions are normally negatively sloped and can shift around, depending on changes in magnitude of the factors which are being held constant along the function. If the function is decreasing, this reflects a lowering of the amount consumers are willing to pay for the same quantity due to changes in the prices of substitutes, complements, income, and so on. The demand function for a good can be increasing over time as well, due to increases in income and population, for example, but these demand increases can be dampened by other factors. In the example given, the other factors causing the demand function to grow less rapidly are costs specific to maintaining slaves in the city, that is, the costs of goods complementary to using urban slaves. Because economists graph demand functions with price on the vertical axis and quantity on the horizontal axis, an increasing demand function moves to the right and a decreasing one to the left.

hands of white laborers when he was hired out as a caulker in Baltimore in 1836. Net incomes from slaves could also have been reduced directly through political avenues by the imposition of taxes, fines, and license fees on slave use.

There is little evidence, however, that white fears were internalized in this manner. Strikes by white workers against slaveowners and attacks on the property of slaveowners were rare. While various license fees and taxes existed, they were very small during the period 1820–60. And between 1850 and 1860, the decade of the greatest decrease in the urban slave population, these taxes and fees remained unchanged in many cities.

There is also reason to doubt the belief held by Wesley and Cairnes that the danger of slave insurrection was greater in the cities than the country, as well as Wade's contention that the cost of controlling urban slaves was rapidly increasing. Although many slave revolts occurred near and in cities prior to the Vesey Conspiracy in Charleston in 1822, most of the insurrections after that date occurred in rural areas.[7] Nor is there any evidence of a substantial increase in slave crimes. This, of course, may have been due to extreme police protection in the cities. But since taxes imposed on slaveowners did not rise over time, such police costs would not affect the rate of change in the demand for slaves.

Another group of writers have argued somewhat differently from those discussed above. They contend not that the urban environment was hostile to slavery but that slaves were more suited for agriculture than for industry. Hence, slaves were more highly desired in the country *relative* to the cities. Some versions of this argument are couched in highly racist tones; others are more rational and will be translated into economic terms.

Although some of Cairnes's ideas have included him in the first group, others put him in the second as well. This does not imply any inconsistency in his thought, for both hypotheses can operate simultaneously. Cairnes asserted that "slave labor is unskillful. . . . Having no interest in his work [the slave] has no inducement to exert his higher faculties. . . . He is therefore unsuited for all branches of industry which require the slightest care. . . . He cannot be made to cooperate with machinery . . . ; he is incapable of all but the rudest forms of labor." Slave labor would thus always be used in one-crop staple production, according to Cairnes, because "the difficulty of teaching the slave anything is so great, that the only chance of turning his labour to profit is, when he has once learned a lesson, to keep him to that lesson for life. . . . If tobacco be cultivated tobacco becomes the sole staple, and tobacco is produced, whatever be the state of the market, and whatever be the condition of the soil."[8]

Both Ulrich B. Phillips and Lewis Cecil Gray concurred with Cairnes's reasoning. Slave labor could only be profitable, wrote Phillips, if "the work required was simple," for then the "shortcomings of Negro slave labor were partially offset by the ease with which it could be organized."[9] Lewis Cecil Gray, with similar racist overtones, believed that the Negro was "primitive" and difficult to control. Thus, the plantation system was adopted because it afforded "more powerful stimuli than the rewards of industry. . . ."[10] Robert Russel, too, focused on the plantation rather than agriculture in general as being the key element in the success of antebellum slavery, for "slaves were better adapted to the routine of the plantation than they were to the more varied tasks of general farming with considerable household manufacturing."[11]

Phillips and some others concluded that slavery's peculiar advantage in staple crop production on plantations was that it enabled economies of scale.† Most writers, without such precise formulations, have recognized that there was something very special about the plantation that was missing from the economic organization of urban slavery.

Another argument for the greater compatibility of slaves in agricultural pursuits is implied by the natural limits thesis. Charles W. Ramsdell, who first formulated the thesis, held that slavery would end after all available lands had been brought into cultivation, for slavery required a continued supply of fresh land to keep up the marginal product of its labor.[12] Thus Ramsdell did not envision slaves as being able to work profitably in cities and industry, because they were inherently an agricultural labor force.

Richard Wade has raised a related issue in his suggestion that the number of slaves who were in the cities between 1820 and 1860 was lower than it would have been if the allocation had been determined purely by profit considerations. But it is by no means

---

†Note that a process or a production function exhibits economies of scale, in an economic sense, if a multiplication of all inputs by some factor, say λ, leads to an increase in output greater than λ.

clear that the allocation of the great bulk of slaves to agriculture was in contradiction with profit maximization. If the South had an enormous comparative advantage in agriculture as compared with the North, profit maximization would have led a greater share of the Southern than the Northern population to reside in rural areas. A more important point is whether the South's comparative advantage in agriculture was related to the existence of slavery or whether it turned only on the South's particular natural endowment. The writers who believed that slavery enabled economies of scale in agriculture which were unavailable in urban work implied that slavery increased the natural advantage that the South already had in agriculture. Therefore the existence of slavery could have retarded Southern urbanization. This is a much larger problem, however, than can be tackled here.[13]

The general difficulty with all the explanations outlined above is that they are too sweeping; they do not explain the considerable variation in the course of urban slavery. They do not help the investigator explain why slavery declined in some cities while it increased in others, and why slavery declined in certain decades while it increased in others. What is required then is an explanation flexible enough to cope with all of the experiences in the cities between 1820 and 1860.

In establishing such an explanation it will be useful to regroup the writers who have been quoted. Those who stated or implied that slavery declined in the cities because of a declining demand for the services of urban bondsmen were actually stating that slaves were *pushed out* of the cities. Cairnes, Douglass, Eaton, Wade, and Wesley all implied that costs of keeping slaves were high in the cities in relation to rural areas and that these costs increased over time. On the other hand, Gray, Phillips, Ramsdell, and Russel, when stressing that slaves were more advantageous in agriculture, were suggesting that if slavery declined in the cities it was due to the *pull* of slaves from cities into staple crop production. This may have been due to a variety of causes, and each of the writers has invoked slightly different ones. I shall define the push hypothesis as stating that the demand for urban slaves was declining, and the pull hypothesis as stating that rural demand increased faster than urban demand. It is possible that both hypotheses were operative at the same time, or that a third, not suggested in the traditional literature, was the correct one.

Whichever factor—push, pull, or another—was functional during this period ought to be detected by certain concomitant changes. If urban demand were declining, one would expect a decline in slave prices for urban slaves. This could be an absolute decline, but it is more likely to have been a decline *relative* to plantation prices for the same workers. Many city slaves had skills specific to urban areas, but the selling price of these slaves to plantations would be equal to that paid for any other field hand. The puzzling feature about an explanation which relies solely on a declining demand for city slaves is that urban slave prices and hire rates continued to rise during the periods 1830–40 and 1850–60, when the equilibrium quantity of slaves in these areas fell dramatically (see tables 16 and 23).

If slaves were being pulled out from the cities, one should expect those slaves with training specific to the cities to remain there, and the less skilled, especially those less skilled in trades specific to the cities, to be sold to the rural areas. If push factors, especially those outlined by Cairnes and Wesley, were operative, we should expect those slaves who were most inimical to urban tranquillity—the skilled and the men—to be sold. The precise movement of these various subgroups depends on the way in which social pressures, if they existed, became internalized. The push and pull theories predict very different changes in the skilled slave populations in the cities.

A more comprehensive explanation must be consistent with all the facts of the period and must be able to predict changes from city to city and from decade to decade. It must come to grips with the fact that the rates of change in the slave populations for the various cities fluctuated in magnitude and even in sign over the four decades. While some urban areas had large decreases, others had large increases in their slave populations. The simple push and pull theories do not enable us to predict these differences. In fact, the push theory is inconsistent with the finding that the heavily industrialized city of Richmond showed increases in its slave population throughout the forty-year period 1820–60. According to a declining demand theory based on control problems, Richmond should have lost slaves as time wore on, since it contained an unusually high proportion of skilled slave labor. This concentration should have created severer problems for Richmond than for other cities.

Moreover, the exodus of slaves from cities seems to have been greater among the unskilled than the skilled (see chapter 3). As 1860 approached, the cities were left with a more highly skilled male labor force than they had had earlier. Unskilled male slaves were sold to the plantations, but the skilled, especially those with skills specific to urban areas, remained in the cities. This, again, is inconsistent with a push theory for the decline in urban slaves. That is, if demand for all types of urban slaves were declining, we would not expect any change in the skill composition of those remaining. Furthermore, if Wade's thesis is correct, if urban masters sold their bondsmen because they no longer felt they had control over them, we again would not expect a change in the male skill mix. Presumably the educated and skilled slaves were more inimical to slavery and hence were more likely to revolt than the uneducated slaves.

Not only were the cities left with a more highly skilled male slave population, but they had more females, especially old ones, and fewer children by the eve of the Civil War than they had had previously. Thus, if the cities pushed their slaves out, they did so with much discrimination. While one might rationalize the greater exodus of unskilled males and children on the grounds that they constituted a more acute threat to safety than skilled males and women, no evidence to support such a view has yet been marshaled.

These considerations make one doubt that the simple versions of the pull and push theories can describe accurately all relevant factors at work during this period. They not only tend to contradict the push hypothesis, but they also suggest that the pull hypothesis is by itself not enough to explain the actual progession of events. Therefore, I shall also consider a third hypothesis: that because of a highly elastic demand for their services,† urban slaves would have been sold from the cities, especially from 1850 to 1860, even if the demand for their services had been increasing at a rate *greater* than that for rural areas. Startling as this alternative hypothesis may seem, it will be shown in chapter 5 that it seems correct for most cities.

†The elasticity of demand measures the responsiveness of changes in quantity demanded to changes in price. The more elastic the demand function, the larger the decrease in quantity demanded, for example, that would result from a price rise.

Although the remainder of this study will demonstrate that slaves were, in part, pulled out from Southern cities, certain urban areas may have suffered declines in slave labor demand during particular decades. In addition, even if the demand for slaves was increasing in the cities, it may have been dampened by factors which were augmenting costs specific to urban areas. It is possible, then, that the costs of holding slaves in cities as opposed to rural areas increased over time as suggested by Wade, Cairnes, and Wesley. But it will be shown that demand declined in very few cities and even for these only in certain decades. It will also be shown that these special urban costs did not rise as rapidly as Wade and others supposed and were, in any case, a small portion of the total cost of slaveholding.

Moreover, while rural demand grew more rapidly than the demand in some cities during some decades, this was not always the case. In most of the forty instances that will be considered, the demand for urban slaves was increasing quite rapidly. In fact, for almost the entire period 1820–60 the growth in demand for urban slaves was greater than the growth in supply. That is, urban areas contributed somewhat to the increase in the price of slaves in general. This claim may appear to be inconsistent with the observed declines in the slave population of various cities, especially between 1850 and 1860. The contradiction is only apparent. It can be resolved by considering the differences between the elasticities of demand in rural and urban areas. Differences in these elasticities also explain fluctuations in the rate of change of the urban slave population.

Questions on the role of slavery in Southern development may, in part, be answered by resolving whether slavery limited the growth of cities and industry—or whether, on the other hand, there were special forces operating in the cities to inhibit the growth of slavery. Therefore, although focusing on changes in urban slave populations, this research also explores the role of slavery in determining the level of urbanization. In addition, it indirectly illuminates the peculiar nature of rural bondage. The crucial aspect of urban slavery, it will be seen, was the greater ability of urban slaveowners to substitute other inputs for slave labor in times of rising slave prices. The fact that rural areas did not have this capacity reinforces the notion that scale economies in the production of staple crops were inherently tied to slave labor.

The Urban Setting of the South

During the period 1820–60, the most populous cities in the South formed what Richard Wade has termed the "urban perimeter." On or close to the sea were Baltimore, Washington, Richmond, Norfolk, Charleston, Savannah, Mobile, and New Orleans. At the northern extreme, on the Mason-Dixon line, were Saint Louis and Louisville (see fig. 1). Within the urban perimeter the South was, for the most part, rural. But toward the end of the slave era this expanse became dotted with small cities and towns such as Augusta, Columbia, Natchez, and Montgomery.

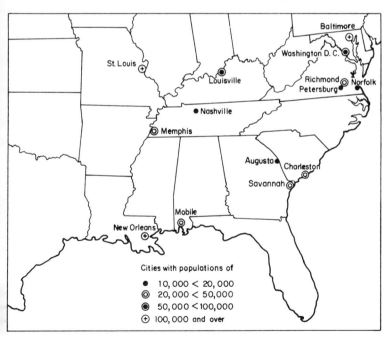

Figure 1. The Urban South: Cities with More Than 10,000 Persons in 1860

The ten cities which composed the urban perimeter always accounted for a major percentage of the urban populations, both white and black. Table 1 shows that in 1850 nine of these cities (Saint Louis excluded) contained 92 percent of all urban whites

TABLE 1   Distribution of White, Free Black, and Slave Populations between Urban and Rural Regions, 1860 and 1850

	White	Free Black	Slave
A. Population (to nearest thousand)			
1850			
9 cities[a]	536,000	55,000	74,000
All urban[b]	580,000	68,000	124,000
Total South[c]	5,630,000	236,000	3,117,000
1860			
9 cities	690,000	58,000	67,000
All urban	713,000	72,000	139,000
Total South	7,034,000	258,000	3,839,000
B. Percentages			
1850			
% of all urban in 9 cities	.92	.81	.60
% of total South in all urban areas	.10	.27	.04
1860			
% of all urban in 9 cities	.97	.80	.48
% of total South in all urban areas	.10	.28	.04

Source: *Federal Population Census*, 1860 and 1850

[a]Saint Louis is excluded (see note b). The nine cities are: Baltimore, Charleston, Louisville, Mobile, New Orleans, Norfolk, Richmond, Savannah, and Washington.

[b]Missouri is excluded because it is impossible to distinguish its cities from its rural areas in the census. "All urban" is defined as Southern cities or towns with an aggregate population exceeding 2,500 and meeting other criteria (see chap. 2, n. 1).

[c]Excludes Missouri. Includes Alabama, Arkansas, Delaware, District of Columbia, Florida, Georgia, Kentucky, Louisiana, Maryland, Mississippi, North Carolina, South Carolina, Tennessee, Texas, and Virginia.

in the South and 60 percent of all urban slaves. In 1860 the same cities accounted for 97 percent of all urban whites but only 48 percent of all urban slaves. Thus, those cities which developed and expanded early in the history of the South contained a majority of the South's total urban population in 1860, although slaves constituted a larger percentage of the population of newer cities.[1]

Much of the business in these Southern cities between 1820 and 1860 was based on commerce. Most of the cities were major ports on the ocean or inland trading routes, involved in the shipping of Southern staple crops to the North and abroad. Few cities were industrial, the most notable exceptions being the Virginia cities of Richmond, Lynchburg, Petersburg, and the large border state cities of Baltimore, Louisville, and Saint Louis. In general, then, the urban region of the antebellum South can be characterized as a service center for a somewhat traditional agricultural economy.

Although these cities were all connected in some way to the agricultural economy on which they bordered, they each differed in size, racial composition, and specific economic activity. Savannah, Charleston, and Norfolk were relatively small ports whose shops catered to the wealthier class of Southern society. Mobile appears to have been supported mainly by the cotton trade, and New Orleans, being the largest of the deep South cities, included the greatest variety of economic activity and social classes. Baltimore, Louisville, Washington, and Saint Louis were very large and diverse, in many ways more like Northern cities. Richmond was the most industrial of the ten; by the 1850s tobacco and iron factories were crowding its first and third wards.

Adult white males in most of the smaller Southern cities were wealthy businessmen, clerks, doctors, lawyers, merchants, railroad men, and shipbuilders, with a substantial percentage owning property, or managing their own businesses. Table 2 gives the occupations of white male adults residing in Savannah and Charleston in 1848. These lists have been presented in their entirety not only because they are interesting but also because the Charleston listing has been incorrectly quoted in several sources.[2] The two cities were probably not typical in that they both appear to have been uniformly wealthy, containing few unskilled whites. The wealth distribution for the three largest cities of the ten in my sample—Baltimore, New Orleans, and Saint Louis—was very unequal. About 85 percent of the wealth in these cities was held by 10

TABLE 2 — Occupations of Free Male Adults in Charleston and Savannah, 1848

A. CHARLESTON[a]
Whites and Free Blacks
(Free Blacks underlined)

Occupation	White	Free Black
1. Contributing to Building		
Bricklayers		_10_
Carpenters	117	_27_
Engineers	43	
Joiners	3	
Lumber dealers	7	
Masons	60	
Painters	15	_4_
Plasterers	9	
Stone cutters	7	
Other	8	
2. Contributing to Clothing		
Boot and shoe dealers	39	
Boot and shoe makers	67	_3_
Cap makers	8	
Clothing dealers	19	
Dry goods dealers	86	_1_
Hat dealers	10	
Hairdressers, barbers	6	_14_
Milliners		_7_
Shoemakers	13	_14_
Tailors	68	_42_
Other	18	
3. Contributing to Education		
Teachers	49	
4. Contributing to Food		
Bakers	35	_1_
Barkeepers	16	
Boarding-house keepers	14	
Butchers	4	_4_
Cooks		_16_
Cigar makers	10	_1_
Confectioners	13	_2_
Farmers	6	
Fishermen	10	_14_
Fruiterers	40	_1_
Gardeners	5	
Grain dealers	8	
Grocers	205	
Millers		_1_
Planters	101	
Restaurant and hotel keepers	5	_1_
Tavern keepers	36	_1_
Other	21	
5. Contributing to Furniture		
Cabinet makers	26	
Carvers and gilders	6	
Crockery dealers	8	
Furniture storekeepers	6	
Gas pipe fitters	8	
Jewelers	17	
Tinners	23	_1_
Upholsterers	10	_1_
Watchmakers	15	
Other	19	
6. Contributing to Health		
Dentists	11	
Druggists	25	
Physicians	89	
Sextons	4	_4_
Undertakers	5	
Other	4	
7. Contributing to Religion		
Clergymen	52	
8. Contributing to Justice		
City officers	35	
Constables	6	
Custom house officers	34	
Keepers of public institutions	8	
Lawyers	76	
Police officers	10	
State officers	11	
Watchmen	90	
Other	28	
9. Contributing to Literature and the Arts		
Actors	7	
Artists	10	
Bookbinders	10	
Book dealers	10	
Editors	5	
Musicians	16	
Painters	11	
Printers	65	
Showmen	5	
Other	14	
10. Contributing to Machinery		
Boiler-makers	6	
Machinists	10	
Millwrights	4	_5_
11. Contributing to Locomotion		
Carriage dealers	8	
Coach makers	10	
Coachmen	2	_4_
Draymen	18	_11_
Harness makers	10	
Railroad clerks	7	
Saddlers	19	_1_
Stable keepers	7	_3_
Wheelwrights	6	_1_
Other	18	
12. Contributing to Navigation		
Navy officers	8	
Pilots	26	
Sail makers	9	
Seamen	150	_1_
Ship carpenters	48	_6_
Wharfingers	20	
Other	18	_1_

TABLE 2—*Continued*

13. Unclassified Mechanics		
Apprentices	56	14
Blacksmiths	45	4
Coopers	20	2
Coppersmiths	5	1
Gunsmiths	6	
Journeymen	4	
Mechanics		2
Other	21	

14. Clerical and Proprietary		
Accountants	98	
Auctioneers	11	
Bank officers	50	
Brokers	21	
Clerks	665	
Collectors	17	
Commission merchants	13	
Factors	49	
Hardware dealers	9	
Merchants	208	
Mill superintendents	14	
Storekeepers	8	5
Wood factors	16	3
Other	16	

15. Unskilled		
House servants	18	9
Hucksters		4
Ironmongers	3	
Janitor		1
Laborers (unspecified)	192	19
Market dealer		1
Peddlers	6	
Porters	8	5

Total Whites   3,943

Total Free Blacks   273

B. SAVANNAH
Whites only

Merchants, factors, and wholesale dealers	263
Planters	50
Shopkeepers and retail grocers	136
Master builders	14
Mechanics[b]	381
Ministers of the Gospel	15
Judges of Courts	4
Physicians	36
Attorneys at Law	31
U.S. Army and Navy officers	6
U.S. civil officers	24
Civil engineer	1
Engineers	30
Clerks[c]	254
Druggists	15

B. (Savannah, cont.)

Pilots	23
Bank officers	24
Teachers	15
Teachers of music	5
Captains of steamers and vessels	28
Captain of the Revenue Service	1
Magistrates	8
County officers	7
Butchers	24
Bakers	22
Boot and shoe makers	27
Printers	14
Connected with railroad	22
Book sellers	3
Watchmakers and jewelers	8
Painters	18
Seamen	58
Manufacturers of tinware	6
Connected with hotels	8
Auctioneers	4
Editors	3
Dentists	4
Artists	2
Lumber measurers	5
Bricklayers	4
Dyers	3
Clothing stores	6
Cigar makers	7
Public stables	4
Barbers	6
Soap and candle manufacturer	1
Engraver	1
Bar rooms	9
Watchmen at banks	4
Saddle and harness makers	5
Millers	6
Connected with steam mills and cotton presses	13
Lumber and wood yards	5
Steamboat yards	9
Lottery offices	2
U.S. soldiers	4
Constables	9
Keepers, sailors' boarding houses	3
Keepers, sailors' home	1
City officers	12
Ice houses	2
Keeper, hospital	1
Jailor and deputy	70
Connected with city watch	70
Laborers (unspecified)	164
Total	1,952

Sources: *Census of the City of Charleston for 1848; Census for the City of Savannah, 1848.*

aThis has been condensed somewhat from the original by the use of an

TABLE 2—*Continued*

"other" category for occupations employing few persons. It has, with few exceptions, been copied directly from the original.

bThis category probably includes carpenters, masons, cabinetmakers, blacksmiths, etc.

cThe term "clerk" refers to both salespersons and office workers.

Comments

The Charleston listing differs from that given by Ulrich B. Phillips, *American Negro Slavery in the United States*, p. 403, because Phillips listed only certain manual occupations.

The term "adult" is not defined in either the Charleston or Savannah censuses. However, the 1848 Charleston census states that "The total number of male whites, in the city, between 20 and 90 years of age were 3,547 for the year ending the first of December, 1848, deducting this amount from the ascertained occupations, 3,923, and there remains 376 under twenty, who are engaged in the various active pursuits of life" (p. 30). Therefore, it appears as if everyone's occupation was ascertained. (The total given in the above quotation is incorrect because of an addition error. The correct figure is 3,943, not, 3,923.) There is a discrepancy between the population figures given in the above quotation and those in the 1850 *Federal Population Census* for white males between 20 and 90. The latter source gives a figure of about 5,600, and the difference can probably be explained by the way in which a suburb called the "Neck" was counted. This same reasoning is used for the free black population of which the 1848 Charleston census states: "The aggregate of free colored males between the ages of 15 and 80 were 298, from this deduct the ascertained occupations, 263, and there remains but 35 whose occupations have not been enumerated" (p. 31). (The total given in the above quotation is incorrect because of an addition error. The correct figure is 273 not 263.)

The white male population over the age of 21 in Savannah was about 2,060 in 1848. This is fairly close to the total figure for occupations of 1,952.

percent of the population, and 40 percent was held by 1 percent. These data display inequalities far exceeding those for the rural South.

Emigration to the South from abroad between 1820 and 1860 was not very great, although most who came to the South went to and remained in the cities. The Border State cities of Baltimore Louisville, and Saint Louis received a large number of the immigrants, with New Orleans, Mobile and Savannah receiving substantial numbers as well (see table 3).[4]

TABLE 3   Percentage of Foreign-Born in the Free Population, 1860

County (City)	Percentage[a]	Adjusted Percentage[b]
Baltimore (Baltimore)	25.0	–
Charleston (Charleston)	20.0	24.6
Jefferson (Louisville)	33.0	41.4
Mobile (Mobile)	26.0	35.7
Orleans (New Orleans)	41.5	42.7
Norfolk (Norfolk)	7.2	•9.9
Henrico (Richmond)[c]	15.3	24.3
Saint Louis (Saint Louis)	52.7	60.3
Chatham (Savannah)	29.0	32.3
Washington (Washington, D.C.)	17.4	21.0

Source: *Federal Population Census*, 1860.

[a]The 1860 *Federal Population Census* does not list data for all cities, but instead gives data for only some cities and all counties. Only the Baltimore data apply to the city. The remaining observations are for the county listed with the corresponding city in parentheses.

[b]To get an upper bound measure of the percentage of foreign-born in the free population of the *city* (not county) I employed the following procedure. I assumed that all foreign-born in the county resided in the city and divided the foreign-born figure by the total free population in the city. This yields a percentage which is more upwardly biased the smaller the city in relation to the county, because in actuality some foreign-born did reside outside the city. This bias is especially acute in the cases of Richmond and Mobile counties, whose cities contained the smallest percentage of the county's free population of those in the table. (See table 18 for the percentage of the free population in each county residing in the city.) The true figure therefore is bounded by the number in the first and second columns. The Baltimore figure was not recomputed, because the city data are given in the first column. The data for Norfolk were computed by dividing the foreign-born in the county by the free populations for both the cities of Norfolk and Portsmouth. This was the only county which contained more than one city. The adjusted percentages are only trivially affected if only free whites are used in the denominator.

Although the true figure is bounded by the data given in these two columns, evidence suggests that the data in the first column are the best proxy. Because we have data for Baltimore city and the county separately, the upper and lower bound figures can be computed for this case, as was done for the other counties. These data are 29.4 and 23.7 percent. The latter figure refers to the first column and is closest to the true figure of 25 per-

TABLE 3—*Continued*

cent, because 19 percent of the free residents of the county were foreign-born.

cHerbert Gutman claims in "The World Two Cliometricians Made," pp. 100–101, that I was incorrect in my doctoral dissertation, "The Economics of Urban Slavery," when I stated that Richmond was not subject to much immigration. But my statement was that Richmond had fewer immigrants as a percentage of its free population *in comparison to the other cities,* and that assertion is correct. Even the adjusted percentages given above, which upwardly bias Richmond's figure, confirm my statement. Gutman bases his argument on the finding that, in 1860, 65 percent of all persons in Richmond who listed their occupation as "laborer" were immigrant whites. But this says nothing about the *aggregate* number of immigrants. It only shows that the nonspecified laboring groups consisted largely of recent arrivals—a finding which one would expect. My conclusions still hold unless one can prove that immigrants who went to other Southern cities competed less with slaves in the labor market than did those in Richmond. Gutman also states that if "the presence (or absence) of immigrant workers is essential to a study of relative urban slave demand 'elasticities,' that thesis is in serious trouble" (p. 101). I do not use the information on immigration to compute these elasticities but employ it in the interpretation of the results (see chapter 5).

Free blacks constituted a large group in most of the cities in my sample,[5] and more than one-quarter of the South's free blacks lived in urban areas. In most cities free blacks were subject to much the same legislation as were slaves. Indeed, although free status allowed them the economic advantage of owning property, it appears that free blacks were far from the top of the economic ladder. The occupational listing in table 2 shows that Charleston's free blacks held a variety of occupations from store owners to servants. But the majority were employed in trades—as tailors, carpenters, bricklayers, and so on. Of those whose occupations were listed in this census, 67 percent were skilled in some trade, suggesting that many of the free blacks were manumitted slaves who had earned their freedom by hiring themselves out. Many may have been escaped bondsmen from other cities, for although most towns prohibited free blacks from entering, these laws were generally ineffective. Southern cities continued to receive many free blacks, and this group remained a large and important part of almost every Southern town.

Slaveowners in the cities were a heterogeneous class, whose occupations and businesses determined how their slaves were employed. Businessmen connected with the railroads, the ports, the shipping trade, and other commercial enterprises owned and hired large numbers of slaves per capita. Commerce, in particular the cotton trade, gave rise to a service sector composed of hoteliers, grocers, lawyers, clerks, and doctors, many of whom also owned and hired slaves. Although most Southern cities did not have large-scale manufacturing, smaller industries such as those connected with the building trades used slaves to meet the needs of the area. Cities were also the second place of residence for some wealthy planters, producing employment for jewelers, clothiers, milliners, and confectioners, who in turn owned slaves.

Census marshals made an obvious attempt in 1860 to list slaves in their place of hire, so that the census manuscript schedules do not necessarily yield information on slave ownership. To account for this problem, I have coined the term "usership," which refers to persons either employing their own slaves or hiring those of others. The 1850 census manuscripts did not distinguish between owners and hirers, and one cannot discern whether a slave listed in that census was included in the owner's or hirer's residence.[6] The 1850 and 1860 usership data, summarized in table 4, show which cities had large and which had small slaveholdings per capita. Owners and hirers in Baltimore, Louisville, Saint Louis, and Washington employed few slaves on average. In fact, over one-half of the total slaves in Baltimore and Washington, D.C., were employed by persons who had only one slave. The majority of these slaves were probably used in domestic activities. In all other cities, except New Orleans, a large percentage of slave employers used substantial numbers of slaves. About one-quarter of Savannah's slave users, for example, listed 10 or more slaves, with some businesses employing very large numbers. Among the largest employers of slaves in that city were the Savannah and Georgia Railroad, and the Central Railroad and Banking Company, each having more than 50. One rice mill employed 55 slaves and a clothing store another 48. Other large users in that city were painters, saddlers, factories, merchants, and physicians.

Mobile and Richmond had similar usership patterns. About one-quarter of their slave-using residents employed only one slave, but 15 percent had 10 or more. Large slaveholdings were common in Richmond, where average slave use in 1860 was 6.6 slaves per slave-using household and business. The bulk of the large

TABLE 4   "Usership" Distribution of Urban Slaves, 1860 and 1850

A. Percentage of Persons Owning or Using Various Numbers of Slaves

	1	2 or 3	4 or 5	6 or 7	8 or 9	10 and above
Baltimore						
1860	50	43	5	2	0	0
1850	62	30	5	2	0	0
Charleston						
1860	9	28	23	16	9	15
1850	21	21	17	12	6	22
Louisville						
1860	44	33	16	4	2	1
1850	29	42	16	8	1	5
Mobile						
1860	20	37	10	12	6	16
1850	27	31	13	12	3	14
New Orleans						
1860	25	37	17	9	5	6
1850	46	25	14	8	1	5
Norfolk						
1860	13	37	19	16	6	10
1850	19	29	24	15	7	7
Richmond						
1860	27	30	13	9	4	17
1850	26	31	11	18	5	8
Saint Louis						
1860	39	39	11	5	3	2
1850	60	23	9	6	1	2
Savannah						
1860	16	20	22	16	4	22
1850	13	11	24	10	15	27
Washington						
1860	59	30	6	5	1	0
1850	61	24	8	4	2	2

B. Average Slave Holdings (of persons who used at least one slave)

	1860	1850		1860	1850
Baltimore	1.72	1.72	Norfolk	4.99	4.53
Charleston	5.97	5.94	Richmond	6.56	5.93
Louisville	2.51	3.29	Saint Louis	2.73	2.50
Mobile	5.95	4.63	Savannah	6.81	7.71
New Orleans	3.72	3.00	Washington	1.89	2.28

Source: *Federal Population Census,* manuscript slave schedules, 1860 and 1850.

"Usership" rather than ownership is given in this table because slaves were distinctly listed by place of employment and not only by owner in the 1860 *Federal Population Census* manuscripts. The definition used in 1850 is unclear, but it is believed that most slaves were counted in their place of employment as in the 1860 census. If this was not the case in Richmond, it may account for Richmond's listing of 17 percent of its slave users as having ten or more slaves in 1860 but only 7 percent having that number in 1850.

users in Richmond were the tobacco factories. One such business, owned by James Grant, employed 132 slaves, and another, operated by T. and S. Hardgrove, listed over 100. Numerous other tobacco manufacturers employed slaves, and probably over 2,000 of Richmond's bondsmen worked in these factories. Artisans, as well, owned and used large numbers of slaves in Richmond. John Quarles, brickmaker and bricklayer, listed about 80 slaves, and James Bosher, a coach manufacturer, had 21.

Commercial activities accounted for many of the large holdings in Mobile. One steamboatman had 140 slaves, and a shipping and commercial merchant used 65. Skilled trades were also common employments for slaves in Mobile, and one carpenter listed 61 slaves.[7]

In Norfolk also, a fairly large number of slave users had 10 or more slaves, with very few having only one. As with Mobile, commerce accounted for many of Norfolk's large slaveholdings. The customs inspector had 40, and the Norfolk Draw Bridge Company, 22. Skilled craftsmen were also large users, with one brickmason employing 40 bondsmen.

New Orleans, being the largest city, is the most difficult to characterize from usership data, for slaves entered all aspects of urban life. A substantial number of New Orleans's slaveholders used from one to three bondsmen, many of whom were probably employed as domestics. But a large percentage of New Orleans's slaves were in big holdings and were employed in a myriad of occupations. The Levee Steam Cotton Press employed 104 slaves, the Front and Tobacco Press used 30, Juan de Egana, a coin merchant, used 42, and a carpenter used 10. Even the Fulton Boys School employed 27 slaves.

By cross-classifying the census manuscript slave schedules (which refer to slave use rather than to slave ownership) with business directories, one can infer with some degree of certainty the occupations of a portion of the slave population. I have employed this technique systematically for a random sample of Savannah's citizens. Where slaveowners and hirers listed fewer than three slaves, one can plausibly surmise that these were employed, at least in part, domestically. With larger numbers it is harder to determine occupation. For example, John Sloan, a butcher, owned or hired 23 slaves, of which 10 were males above ten years old. Although some of these slaves were probably engaged in the butchering trade, one cannot be certain how many Sloan used in his home and how many in his business.

Physicians had many slaves, a great percentage of whom were women. Dr. James M. Schley, for example, owned or hired 19 slaves, of whom seven were females above the age of 10. Some probably aided in the doctor's practice. Merchants and clerks listed large holdings of slaves. William H. Gibbons, whose occupation was given as clerk, had 52 slaves, and George W. Davis, a commission merchant, 19. Other clerks and merchants also had larger-than-average holdings, partly a function of their wealth but possibly also due to their using slaves in their businesses. Only a few owners of slaves in the city listed their occupations as planter. That is, almost all of the slaves residing in the city worked in urban employments, and only a trivial number were actually part of the agricultural work force. A complete summary of these data can be found in table 5.

The extent of slave usership, in terms of the percentage of the white population using slaves, seems to have been determined by a number of important variables. It was partly the result of the distribution of urban wealth. It also reflected the extent of slave labor substitutes in the various cities. Table 6 shows that percentages of white males over 19 years old who employed slaves varied considerably across cities, with Norfolk attaining a high of 44 percent in 1850 and Saint Louis a low of 1 percent in 1860.

The percentage of white males over 19 years old who hired and owned slaves in the cities declined between 1850 and 1860. Part of this drop was due to an increase in the number of free whites, and part to the decline in the urban slave population. Erosion in slave use is most apparent in Charleston, Mobile, Norfolk, and Richmond. In each of these cities slave use was widespread in 1850. In three of them, more than 40 percent of the white male adults owned or hired slaves in 1850. By 1860, this number had dropped to between 20 and 30 percent. These dramatic changes in slave use ought to be reflected in the laws that were passed and enforced during this decade, which does seem to be the case for Richmond (see chapter 3 and the Appendix, pages 133–38). But although the data for all cities show a decrease in urban slave use, most of the 1860 figures are still quite substantial. These changes may have been the result of an increase in adult white

TABLE 5 Occupations of Slaveowners and Slave Hirers in Savannah, 1860

Occupation of Slaveowner and/or Hirer[a]	Number of Slaves			Occupation of Slaveowner and/or Hirer[a]	Number of Slaves		
	Males ≥ 10 Years	Females ≥ 10 Years	Children ≤ 9 Years		Males ≥ 10 Years	Females ≥ 10 Years	Children ≤ 9 Years
Agent for railroad	8	3	4	Clerk	1	1	0
Attorney	1	6	2	"	0	1	0
"	4	2	0	"	15	19	18
"	2	3	0	Wife of above Clerk	1	1	0
"	1	5	2	Collection clerk	1	1	4
"	1	1	0	"	9	7	3
"	0	1	2	Commercial merchant	0	1	0
Wife of above Attorney	0	3	3	"	10	9	9
Baker	2	0	0	"	2	1	4
"	7	2	0	"	1	0	1
Bookkeeper for railroad	0	1	1	"	2	1	1
Bookkeeper	4	10	5	Commission merchant	6	6	7
"	9	12	2	Customs house	4	4	5
Brickmason	0	3	0	Druggist	0	1	0
Broker	11	9	3	"	2	1	0
Butcher	10	8	5	"	2	1	0
Cabinetmaker	0	2	0	Dry goods	0	2	2
Captain of towboat	5	2	0	Editor of Savannah Republican	1	2	3
Captain of schooner	1	0	0	Feed and hides	6	3	1
Carpenter	1	1	0	Greengrocer	0	1	0
"	5	2	4	Grocer	1	1	0
Cigars and tobacco	0	1	2	"	1	5	0
City treasurer	4	1	0	"	0	1	0
Clerk	1	4	0	"	0	3	0
				"	0	0	1

TABLE 5—*Continued*

Occupation of Slaveowner and/or Hirer[a]	Number of Slaves			Occupation of Slaveowner and/or Hirer[a]	Number of Slaves		
	Males ≥ 10 Years	Females ≥ 10 Years	Children ≤ 9 Years		Males ≥ 10 Years	Females ≥ 10 Years	Children ≤ 9 Years
Grocer	0	0	1	Wife of Physician	9	7	3
"	1	3	1	President of railroad[b]	155 slaves in total		
Jail - slaves in jail	9	2	0	Rice mill superintendent	1	1	0
Lawyer	1	2	1	Saddle and harness manufacturer	1	1	1
Lumber and brick merchant	2	3	0	"	1	0	0
Machinist, iron brass foundries	4	2	1	Salesman	0	1	2
Master machinist	1	1	1	Saloonkeeper	1	2	2
Merchant	2	5	4	Sheriff of Chatham County	3	7	2
"	2	0	0	Stave machinist	8	7	9
Milliner	0	1	0	Superintendent of dry dock	0	1	0
Notary and commissioner of deeds	2	2	0	Tailor	0	1	0
Poultry dealer	2	3	1	Timber factors	1	0	0
Physician	0	2	1	Watches and jewelry	1	0	0
"	4	7	8	Wheelwright and blacksmith	0	1	0
"	3	3	1				
"	6	5	1				
"	0	3	0				

Sources: *Federal Population Census*, manuscript slave schedules, 1860. Savannah Business Directory, 1860.

[a]I sampled one out of every eight pages of the 1860 manuscript slave schedules of Savannah. This yielded 131 slaveowners and hirers, for which I could find the occupations of 80 in the Savannah business directory. Many of the owners and hirers whose occupations could not be found were females. The occupation given was copied directly from the directory.

[b]These slaves belong to the estate of James P. Screven, who was a railroad president in 1859. Relatives of Screven, also residing in Savannah's 4th District and holding over 100 slaves, are listed as planters in the business directory.

TABLE 6   Urban Slaveowners and Slave Hirers as a Percentage of
Urban White Males Twenty Years of Age or Older,
1860 and 1850

ity	1860	1850
altimore	3%	4%
harleston	29	59
ouisville	11	15
obile	19	35
ew Orleans	12	16
orfolk	26	43
ichmond	26	40
avannah	24	30
aint Louis	1	4
ashington	7	12

Sources: Table 4, part B (above); *Federal Population Census*, 1860 and 1850.

I have assumed that only white males over nineteen years old used slaves. That is, if a family owned or hired slaves, they are assigned to the male in the household. To the extent that slave users included some white females and free blacks, the resulting figures are overestimates of the percentage of free white males owning or hiring slaves. I have chosen this method because I am interested in ascertaining the relative political power of slaveowners, and white males appear to have been the only political force in these Southern cities. In addition, the changes over time in this variable should not be affected by this method of computation.

males in the lower part of the wealth distribution—and not a reflection of the political strength of urban slave users.

The percentage of the male labor force in each of the cities who were employed in manufacturing (see table 7) enables one to categorize these cities on the basis of their internal composition. Most of the cities were not large manufacturing centers. Some of the largest, in both absolute and relative size, were Border State cities which contained few slaves in their manufacturing labor forces. Richmond was an obvious outlier in terms of industrial activity, and other evidence shows that bondsmen were extensively used in Richmond's manufacturing sector.

TABLE 7   Manufacturing in Southern Cities, 1860

County (City)	Percentage of Male Population 15 to 60 Years Old Employed in Manufacturing	
Baltimore (Baltimore)	6.1%	(3,547/57,929)[a]
Charleston (Charleston)	5.0	(908/18,025)
Jefferson (Louisville)	23.1	(6,316/27,342)
Mobile (Mobile)	4.1	(598/14,585)
Orleans (New Orleans)	8.8	(5,057/57,316)
Norfolk (Norfolk)	6.3	(644/10,174)
Henrico (Richmond)	53.9	(7,418/13,763)
Saint Louis (Saint Louis)	16.7	(10,923/65,542)
Chatham (Savannah)	1.7	(174/10,235)
Washington (Washington, D.C.)	12.9	(2,653/20,528)

Source: *Federal Manufacturing and Population Censuses*, 1860. Count data have been used since city data were unavailable.

[a]Figures in parentheses are the raw data, that is, the number of males i manufacturing divided by the number of males between fifteen and sixt years old.

The census manuscript schedules for 1860 list 52 tobacco man ufacturers in Richmond, most of whom either hired or owne slaves as their primary laboring force. One-sixth of the total mal labor force of Henrico County, which contains Richmond, wa engaged in tobacco manufacturing. The same figure applies t Campbell County, which contains Lynchburg.[8] Throughout all c Virginia, tobacco factories hired about 40 percent of their slav labor force in 1850; by 1860 the proportion had increased t about 50 percent.[9] Richmond's factories appear to have relie even more heavily on hired slaves. The factories in its first war the center of Richmond industry, hired 87 percent of their slave in 1860.[10] Although it is difficult to determine the total numbe of slaves who worked in industrial establishments in the urba South, the census manuscripts show that about one-third of Rich mond's adult male slaves were used in tobacco and iron produc tion. Lynchburg, developing somewhat later than Richmond, ha 47 tobacco factories in 1860, 18 flour mills, and 4 iron factorie all of which used slaves extensively.

It is not clear why the Border State cities lacked large industrial
nd commercial holdings of slaves. For example, Baltimore, Saint
Louis, and Washington never had the large slave holdings that
ther cities had. Perhaps this is due to their location close to freedom, or possibly to their northern climate, which helped attract
n abundance of immigrants. The empirical work in chapter 4
ends credence to the latter hypothesis.

Most large Southern cities served as centralized markets for the
lave trade. New Orleans, Richmond, and Charleston were large
lave trading centers, Charleston being important especially during
he pre-embargo period of slavery. Smaller cities were also in-
olved in this trade. Natchez, for example, which developed dur-
ng the boom period of the West South Central region, was a filter
or slaves coming from the Old to the New South.

Urban slavery was a multi-faceted institution in the antebellum
outh. If one were to have visited the Border State cities of Balti-
nore and Washington toward the end of the antebellum era, one
ould have thought of urban slavery as synonymous with the em-
loyment of black female domestics. But traveling a little further
outh to Richmond and Lynchburg, one would have gotten the
npression that slave labor supported all the industry in the South.
 trip even further to Charleston, Mobile, and Savannah would
ave led one to believe that the entire commercial traffic of the
outh was managed by slaves. In each city one would have been
truck by the variety of occupations in which slaves were em-
loyed. The differences among the cities will become more impor-
nt as the course of slavery in these cities is described and
nalyzed.

3   Life in the Cities

It is difficult to characterize the general milieu of Southern cities, for the daily routine of the inhabitants of industrial Richmond, for example, appears to have been as different from that of Savannah as from that of a Northern city. Certain characteristics, however, were common to all urban areas in the South.

In all Southern cities, slaves were a prominent feature of the economy. They had similar occupations, were confined by analogous laws, and were held in a bondage that underwent similar changes. In addition, the relationship between whites and slaves in every city was an intricate one which ultimately pitted white against white during the period studied. In each city, owners of slaves attempted to protect their investments against the designs of the white artisan and laboring classes.

This chapter focuses only on those features of the urban slave system most important to an economic inquiry. In particular, the development of economic institutions relating to slavery and the social interactions among the cities' inhabitants will be examined. For a more complete picture of urban slave life, the reader is advised to consult Richard C. Wade's *Slavery in the Cities*.

The Relationship between Whites and Slaves

In most of the cities in the antebellum South, ownership and other forms of financial interest in slavery were widespread (see table 4). Slave interests, therefore, were usually well represented in the city councils, the law-making bodies of these towns. But throughout the period 1820–60, white tradesmen and artisans attempted to close their occupations to slave labor. These skilled workers saw that their livelihoods could be advanced by the placing of heavy restrictions on slave employment. They petitioned city councils for ordinances prohibiting the use of slave labor in various occupations. In addition, they spread propaganda in certain city newspapers about the alleged evils of using slaves in skilled positions. Many of the incompatibility arguments advanced in chapter 1 appear to find their origin in these white artisan campaigns. But because of the large numbers both of slaveowners and of hirers of slaves (see table 6), only a handful of the laws drafted by the artisans ever found their way into the ordinance books of the cities. Thus, slaves were politically represented, to some degree, through the voting strength of their owners and hirers.

Examples of these artisan petitions are legion. They appeared early in the history of the cities and continued until the 1860s. They were sometimes successful but more often not. The butchers of Savannah, for example, formed a committee and entered a petition in the Minutes of Council in 1822 "to prevent slaves from butchering and selling meats in the Market on their own account and for their individual benefit." The reasons given for this restriction were that the market place afforded slaves "facilities . . . to sell small meats . . . unfairly acquired."[1] Although it is not clear what became of the many petitions drafted by the butchers, in 1842 they again were lobbying for "an ordinance to exclude from the Market House colored persons as buyers and sellers of meat."[2] Eventually the city fathers partly yielded to this pressure, for a law concerning slave butchers appears in the *Ordinances of the City of Savannah* for 1854. "[N]o slave shall act as butcher," the law reads, "unless in the presence of the owner, employer, or employers, or his, her or their agent, being a white person."[3] This may have limited competition from slave butchers, but it far from eliminated them from the meat market.

The tradesmen of Charleston, from time to time, also petitioned their legislature to prohibit certain slave activities. Most important of the laws actually passed were those prohibiting slaves from hiring out their own time. But these laws became, in the words of the South Carolina Mechanic Association of Charleston, "a dead letter." This group petitioned in 1858 for a law which would subject "to indictment both the hirer as well as the owner of any slave hiring out time." They further requested a tax on free persons of color so "that we may be able to compete with them."[4]

In Richmond, skilled puddlers working in the iron industry expressed their distaste for black competition in a resolution stating that they "would not go to work, unless the negroes be removed from the puddling furnace at the new mill, likewise from the squeezer and rolls in the old mill" (*Richmond Enquirer*, 29 May 1847). The strike which ensued in Anderson's Tredegar ironworks was short-lived, for Anderson decided to do without his recalcitrant white laborers. Although his action created quite a stir in the white community, some believed that Anderson's response was not to be condemned. The *Enquirer*, in expressing this sentiment, noted that an attempt to reverse Anderson's decision would "render slave property utterly valueless and place employers in the power of their employed" (ibid.).[5] Once again, those who had financial interests in slave use protected their investments, heightening divisions between the white propertied and nonpropertied classes.

Another method by which slave use in the cities was limited was the imposition of wage laws, which set minimum payment that could be made to a slave. If the payment were set high enough, it could thwart competition between whites, whose wages were uncontrolled, and slaves. A few cities had such legislation. Charleston, in 1837, set wage minima for porters and day laborers at one dollar for a full day's labor, and Norfolk passed an ordinance in 1845 stating that slaves who were hired out were "entitled to receive the sum of one dollar for every day while employed."[6]

The enmity between white and slave laborers occasionally took the form of brutality. It was mentioned in chapter 1, for example, that Frederick Douglass was severely beaten when hired out as a caulker. "The white laboring man was robbed by the slave system of the just results of his labor," Douglass wrote, "because he was flung into competition with a class of laborers who worked without wages."[7] This economic rationale was to Douglass the main source of discontent, and there is no doubt that his experience was not unique.

The artisans and tradesmen of the Southern cities did not win in their bid for increased economic gain. They were frustrated in their attempts by the voting strength of those desiring to protect their property in slaves. These white laboring classes therefore turned their attention toward restricting the occupational opportunities of the free black, who was far weaker politically. The white mechanics of Richmond, for example, organized in 1857 to prevent free blacks from becoming mechanics. They made it clear that "we do not aim to conflict with the interest of slave owners, but to elevate ourselves as a class from the degrading positions which competition with those who are not citizens of the commonwealth entails upon us" (*Richmond Enquirer*, 27 August 1857). Free Negroes were already prohibited from becoming "doctors, lawyers, merchants, [and] tradesmen," and the mechanics desired to extend these restrictions.

Artisans and tradesmen were not the only groups attempting to restrict the use of slave labor, for bondsmen were competitors of unskilled immigrant workers too. In New Orleans, dock strikes by unskilled workers, mainly recent arrivals from Ireland and Germany, were broken by slave "scab" labor. Considerable violence accompanied these labor conflicts in the early 1850s. For a time, blacks were excluded from the wharves by "labor racketeers," as the newspapers termed them. But a law passed in 1858 made such exclusion illegal and also legislated against picketing. The use of slaves as strike breakers was common in Southern towns and surely accounted for some of the animosity between slaves and poor whites.

Although most of the petitions drafted by the tradesmen of the various cities were for greater restrictions on slaves, some sought to ease certain restrictions. Merchants had an economic interest in slaves, not because they owned or hired them, but because they sold goods to them. Slaves were not merely workers in the cities, they were also consumers. In 1817 the merchants and storekeepers of the town of Camden, South Carolina, petitioned the state legislature to revise a law which required slaves to have written permission to purchase goods for their owners. Claiming that "the law as it stands serves to prohibit trade between slaves and retailers,"[8] the storekeepers requested that the law be changed to allow slaves to purchase between one and five dollars' worth of merchandise for their own or their owner's use without written permission.

A similar petition was heard in the Savannah city council in 1835. The grocers and traders of that city requested a change in the hours during which slaves were permitted to trade. Under the existing legislation, slaves from neighboring farms marketed crops, which they produced in their spare time, in Savannah. They were allowed to sell their produce on Sunday, although the market was closed to all other business. This legislation was opposed by the grocers and traders of the city because "it presupposes that [a slave] comes to the city on one day to sell and on another to buy."[9] The petition requested that Saturday rather than Sunday afternoon be the day for rural slaves to market their produce in the city so that they could purchase as well.

Even though there were many laws prohibiting trade and socializing between slaves and whites, these activities continued in the cities probably to a greater extent than in the country. There were more opportunities for whites and slaves to intermingle in the cities, with their backroom bars and gambling establishments. There was, of course, money to be made in selling liquor to slaves, but many accounts indicate that the city fostered genuine friendships between slaves and whites.

The minutes of the Charleston Court of General Sessions show that numerous whites were found guilty of selling liquor to slaves. Ordinarily the harshest penalty in the late 1850s was a hundred-dollar fine and six months in jail. But in 1860 the court attempted to curtail the trade by increasing fines to the staggering sum of one thousand dollars and jail sentences to nine months. In 1861, however, the court reverted to lower fines and from one to six months in jail.

One may wonder how slaves received income with which to engage in gambling, drinking, and ordinary trade with whites. Certainly some slaves must have been given allowances, as is clear from the accounts of Richmond tobacco factories. Many slaves hired themselves out (though payment for their time went mainly to their masters), and some probably did odd jobs in their spare time to earn extra money for themselves. We know from the Richmond tobacco factories that supplemental payment was given directly to the slaves as a reward for good work or overtime.[10] There may also have been trade in stolen goods in the cities, with slaves playing the part of the middleman. The Grand Jury of Charleston noted—though we do not know how accurately or impartially—that "quite a number of low drinking houses have been established just without the corporate limits of the city. . . . It is to these dens of iniquity that our slaves resort at night and on Sunday, with stolen property to be exchanged for poisonous strychnine whiskey. . . . Quite a number of small establishments have been reported as engaged in the sale of lottery tickets and the slaves are their best customers."[11]

Thus the relationship between slaves and whites was complex. One out of every four adult white males owned or hired slaves in Mobile, Norfolk, Richmond, Savannah, and Charleston in 1860. Although the percentage of adult white males who used slaves was smaller in other cities, it was larger for all cities in 1850. Even if these users had no direct interest in slave property, many desired to keep the system viable for other reasons. They vigorously protected the rights of slave owners to invest in their bondsmen's training and to hire them out in various occupations. They guaranteed through their political lobbying that slaveowners and hirers could decide where their slaves would live and how their payment was to be determined.

It is not an easy task to separate the economic interests of a vocal lobbying group from the true feelings of the populace. Newspapers frequently reported daily legislative activity without noting which groups initiated the petitions. There were certainly differences of opinion on these matters within the white community, but it is important to discern the voice of the majority. The legislative petitions that resulted from the reaction to the Vesey Plot, for example, probably reflected the real anxieties of some citizens of Charleston.[12] But, in general, the people of Charleston and other Southern cities could not believe that their trusted servants, many of them skilled artisans, would ever rebel. Most of the restrictive legislation suggested during the early 1820s in Charleston never entered the ordinance books.[13] Thus, it appears that the majority of urban citizens in the antebellum South did not consider slaves to be dangerous enough to legislate vigorously against them. (See Appendix for a summary of the slavery laws that were passed in Southern cities.)

The Relationship between Free Blacks and Slaves

There were numerous complaints in all Southern cities about free blacks' socializing with and harboring slaves, and there were many who desired to put an end to all social and economic relationships between slaves and their free friends. Most vociferous in this campaign were some slaveowners who believed that such socializing was a major cause of slave idleness. Mayor Joseph Mayo of Richmond, in a report to the city council in 1853, stated that "much good may be accomplished by preventing all intercourse between slaves and free Negroes, especially in the night."

He suggested an ordinance which would punish "a free Negro who will permit a slave to be on his lot of tenement between sunset and sunrise, with or without the leave of the owner, or in the day time, except by written authority of the owner." This was believed to be "the best mode of stopping board money, cook shops, and eating houses, the hiring of slaves by free Negroes, (a great evil)" (*Richmond Enquirer*, 10 August 1853).

The list of undesirable practices given by Mayor Mayo illustrates the extent of slave freedoms within Richmond. Board money was given by individuals and manufacturing establishments to both hired and personally owned slaves in lieu of provisions. This custom resulted in eating houses and cook shops for slaves, and some slaves also secured their own housing. It appears that free blacks provided these services, for as free citizens they could own property.

The problem of runaways made whites suspicious of contacts between slaves and free blacks. Free blacks occasionally harbored runaway slaves, provided them with false identification, and gave them funding to travel to the North. The *New Orleans Daily Picayune* in 1858 (6 October) described an organization of free blacks and slaves which arranged for the transference of papers from exbondsmen in northern cities to those still enslaved in New Orleans.

Free blacks also helped slaves in furthering their education. Many of the free black caulkers with whom Frederick Douglass worked could read and write, and they had organized a society for their mental improvement. It was through these free black friends that Douglass advanced his own education. "I had on the Eastern Shore been only a teacher when in company with other slaves," wrote Douglass, "but now there were colored persons here who could instruct me."[14]

Free blacks, although able to own property and hold managerial positions, were subject to almost all the legal restrictions which bound slaves. Thus they could sell housing and other amenities to slaves and, at the same time, were brought closer to their black friends by their similar position in society. They prayed in the same churches, they frequented the same eating and drinking places, and, most importantly, they intermarried.

Economic Aspects of Urban Slave Life

Many who have written on urban slavery have noted that urban slaves had more freedoms than their rural counterparts. Recent work on plantation slavery, however, has shown how plantation slaves, as well, could temper the rigor of their environment.[15] Institutions such as hiring out also developed in rural areas. Still, the cities allowed the development of more complex arrangements. Not only were urban slaves hired out, but many, as we have seen, lived apart from their place of work.[16] These slaves were allowed to locate their own place of residence and buy their own meals. Slaves socialized both among themselves and with their free friends.

The important question is whether these changes in slave life enhanced the profitability of the institution or signaled its demise. Probably the most important contribution to the economic survival of slavery in its urban environment was the practice of slave hiring. The cities became major slave-hiring centers for their own as well as the surrounding rural community. If the owner of a slave carpenter, for example, did not have sufficient work to keep his slave occupied for the entire year, he could hire out the remainder of the slave's services to other persons. Although slaves were typically hired for a full year, guardianship accounts for Fredericksburg, Lynchburg, Richmond, and Savannah show that 30 percent of those slaves hired out by their owners were contracted for periods less than one year.[17] Hiring was more common in the cities than elsewhere (see table 8), because the more extensive urban markets reduced the transactions costs of renting.

The 1860 manuscript slave census gives information on slave hiring that varies from state to state in its reliability. The census marshals appear to have been instructed to report not merely the owner but also the person who was hiring each slave, though marshals in some states were negligent in compiling these statistics. For example, the hiring data for urban areas in Virginia appear to be quite complete, while similar data for Louisiana are too sparse to be accepted. The numbers that appear in table 8 are to be taken as lower bounds because many slaves who were hired were probably not listed as such.[18] Nevertheless, the data show that hiring was quite common in the cities, especially in the more industrial centers of Virginia such as Richmond, Norfolk, Ports-

TABLE 8   Slave Hiring in Five Southern Cities and Rural
               Virginia, 1860

City or Region	Percentage of Slave Population Hired		Percentage of Slave Labor Force Hired[b]	
	Male	Female	Male	Female
Louisville	24	27		
Lynchburg	52	35		
Portsmouth	38	38	50[c]	52[c]
Richmond	62	38	71[d]	46[d]
Washington	15	19		
Rural Virginia[a]	6	5	7[c]	5[c]

Source: *Federal Population Census*, manuscript slave schedules, 1860.
   [a]Bedford, Halifax, Buckingham, and Princess Ann Counties.
   [b]This figure has not been computed for all cities.
   [c]The labor force is defined here as the population between fifteen and
fifty years old.
   [d]The labor force is defined here as the population between ten and fifty
years old.

mouth, Lynchburg, and Fredericksburg. Hiring appears to have
developed to its greatest extent in these cities. Richmond alone
had eighteen hiring agents, whose job was to find temporary employment for slaves and to board them if necessary during the
period of search. The basic fee paid to these agencies was between
5 and 8 percent of the yearly hire, and other services, such as
boarding and medical attention, were extra.[19] Even slaves working
for the rural Dismal Swamp Land Company were hired through
Richmond agents.[20] Mobile had special stands in various parts of
the city, where slaves who hired themselves out by the day could
meet prospective buyers.

An interesting aspect of urban slave hiring is that it enabled
especially efficient use of very young and old labor. It can be seen
in table 9 that the distribution of ages for hire in Richmond was
quite similar to that for the entire slave population. This implies
that the children of hired slaves were not separated from their parents, and that older persons were employed, perhaps as part of a
family package. The sex distribution of hires, unlike the age distribution, did not correspond to that for the entire slave population,

TABLE 9   Age Distributions for All Richmond Slaves and for Hired
Richmond Slaves, 1860

	0-9	10-19	20-29	30-49	50-59	60 and over
A. Total Richmond Slaves: Percentage of Population in Age Category[a]						
Males	18 (13[b])	26	20	27	5	4
Females	24 (21[b])	24	17	23	7	6
B. Hired Richmond Slaves: Percentage of Population in Age Category						
Males	7	30	22	32	5	3
Females	11	29	19	29	8	4

Source: *Federal Population Census*, manuscript slave schedules, 1860, for
Virginia and Henrico County.
[a]This age distribution is for Henrico County and is somewhat different
from that given in table 15.
[b]The percentage in this age group is for the city of Richmond. See table
15.

at least in the more industrial cities (see table 8). Richmond and
Lynchburg hired more males than females as a percentage of their
available slave labor. Male slaves in these cities appear to have
worked in the factories while their wives stayed in the master's
house and worked as domestic servants. In cities such as Louisville and Washington, where most slaves worked in domestic or
unskilled positions, hiring percentages between the sexes were
more similar.

Slaves employed as house servants and factory workers were
usually hired by a yearly contract. Tradesmen were more often
hired for short periods, probably by the job. Most contracts, regardless of duration, specified the period of hire, the net hire rate
(i.e., the payment to be made to the slaveowner—not a wage
payment, since room, meals, and clothing were paid for by the
hirer), and the goods which the hirer was to provide the slave at
the end of the period. The latter typically included a suit or more
of clothing, possibly shoes and stockings, and almost always a
blanket. Most contracts did not include provisions for medical
care, but guardianship accounts show that the hirer was liable for
such expenses although not for the possible death of the slave.

Many owners who hired their slaves out for especially risky occupations, such as work on the railroad, took out life insurance policies on them.[21]

Toward the beginning of the period 1820–60, and even earlier, many Southern cities began requiring that hired slaves either wear metal identification badges or be registered with the city clerk. In Mobile, New Orleans, Norfolk, and Richmond this involved either no payment or a small fee and appears to have been conceived more for control than for revenue raising and restriction. Mobile, in 1843, and Norfolk, in 1845, required a one-dollar yearly fee for a hiring license or badge. New Orleans made badges mandatory in 1817 with no specified fee, and Richmond required as early as 1806 that slaves hired by the year be registered.[22] Both Savannah and Charleston had more substantial badge fees, which were graduated by the slave's skill level. Savannah required, in 1839, that slaves working as mechanics, cabinetmakers, house or ship carpenters, caulkers, bricklayers, blacksmiths, tailors, barbers, bakers, and butchers have badges costing about ten dollars apiece; badges for other occupations were less expensive. This law was amended in 1857 to exempt slaves who were hired from one Savannah family to work in the home of another. Charleston's hiring ordinances, initiated in 1806, were similar to Savannah's, with skilled trades costing more than unskilled occupations.[23]

The badge systems seem to have served a variety of purposes. In a few cities, badge fees were obviously a method of raising revenues. Charleston raised almost one-tenth of its 1849 city taxes by this means.[24] Badges may also have been an attempt to placate white artisans, as fee schedules suggest. In general, however, badges and other forms of registering were intended to control slave hiring. For example, the Savannah city council resolved in 1812 that, "[n]o more badges [are] to be issued 'negro wenches' for the sale of fruit because of want of nurses."[25] In addition, the wearing of a badge made it easier to spot runaways and slaves who did not belong in certain parts of town. Whatever the reasons behind the system, it involved only trivial costs in all but two of the cities examined. It appears to be of minor importance in answering why slavery did not flourish in the cities.

Many slaves, especially those who were skilled, hired out their own time. The owners of these slaves found it more profitable to allow them to find their own work. Slaves who self-hired paid their owners some fraction of their earnings, usually by the month, and most slaves who hired their own time worked in their owner's city. But some who engaged in self-hire were employed many miles from their owners, who often instructed friends or relatives to look after them. One South Carolina slaveowner named Bell, who lived in Beaufort, had slaves who hired themselves out thirty miles away in Savannah. Bell wrote his cousin William Garland in Savannah: "Jimmy . . . and Tom . . . are going to Savannah to work out, will you be kind enough and protect them if anything may occur that will want a white person's interference. . . . In fact I wish you would take them under your charge while in Savannah."[26]

Most Southern cities legislated against the practice of self-hire, but it was difficult to enforce such legislation. Self-hire appears to have continued at least until 1860 in most of the cities studied. Richmond had prohibited self-hire by 1859. By 1854, Savannah had restricted the self-hiring of mechanics, unless written permission was given by the slaveowner. Mobile's history of self-hire legislation shows much ambiguity; it was illegal in 1828, legal with restrictions in 1843, and illegal again in 1858.[27]

At the state level, some legislation concerning self-hire existed throughout the South. Virginia in 1782 was the first to pass such laws, with a prohibition against slaves' hiring out their own time, and all other slave states followed suit. Texas' law in 1846 was the last in this series. Georgia prohibited self-hire of slaves in 1803 but exempted slaves in the towns of Savannah, Augusta, and Sunbury. Alabama had a similar ruling in 1805, which was made more comprehensive in 1848.[28]

Self-hire permitted the slave a considerable degree of freedom. Many bondsmen earned sizable sums,[29] and the reduction in transaction costs made possible by self-hire meant gains for both slave and master. Some enterprising slaves even hired out other slaves. For example, a slave carpenter hiring out his own time might employ slave helpers hired within the city. Mobile's legislation of 1858 specifically stated that slaves could not hire the time of other slaves, and an 1848 Charleston ordinance provided that slaves who worked for other slaves must wear badges.[30]

Violations of self-hire ordinances were common. The General Assembly of Kentucky outlawed self-hire in 1802, but the *Louisville Public Advertiser* reported in 1820 (24 June) that "in direct

opposition to this law there are *at least 150 slaves* . . . in this town
—some of whom pay their 'owners' twenty dollars per month,
others at the age of 70 pay nine or ten dollars per month—female
slaves pay from four to six dollars and support three or four children each" (my italics). It is important to note that 150 adult
slaves constituted over 20 percent of Louisville's slave labor force
in 1820. Again in 1827 (10 November) the same newspaper reported further campaigns against "slaves who [go] at large and
[hire] themselves." A female slave who broke the law in 1850,
according to the *Louisville Daily Courier Journal* (29 May 1850),
was sentenced to three months in the workhouse. Given an average net hire rate of thirty-two dollars for females in 1850, this
infraction cost the slaveowner eight dollars plus jail fees. A letter
written to the *Charleston Courier* in 1850 (12 September) complained that, even with a new law in effect, "not one slave less
hires his time than before."

Living Out Arrangements

Many hired slaves lived apart from their employers. Although
there are no precise estimates of the percentage of slaves not living
with their owner or hirer, the *Census of the City of Charleston for
the Year 1861* allows an indirect computation. This census, which
is partially summarized in Table 10, reported information on the
owner, occupant, construction, and ward location of every building in the city. About one in thirteen of Charleston's residential
structures was occupied solely by slaves in 1861, and one in twelve
by either slaves or both free blacks and slaves living together. If
the implied average number of free blacks per house (9.7) is used
as an estimate for the slave structures, then 15 percent of all
slaves, that is one in seven, lived apart from their owners.[31] Some
of these slaves may have lived in buildings adjoining that of their
master, but these structures had to be separate entities to have
been included in this census. Table 10 also shows that only 5
percent of the slaves lived in brick structures, as opposed to 37
percent of the whites. These data make it clear that blacks tended
to live in some Charleston wards rather than in others; 18 percent
of the Sixth Ward's houses, for example, were occupied by blacks,
although only 2 percent of those in the First Ward were.

Almost all cities legislated in some way against the institution
of living out, just as they did against hiring practices. In both

TABLE 10   Numbers of Houses Occupied by Slaves, Free Blacks, and Whites Living in Charleston's Eight Wards, 1861

	Ward Number							
	1	2	3	4	5	6	7	8
Slaves								
Brick houses	0	2	6	2	0	0	0	0
Wood houses	6	6	24	20	22	78	6	30
Slaves and Free Blacks[a]								
Brick houses	0	0	0	0	0	0	0	0
Wood houses	0	0	2	2	12	0	0	0
Free Blacks								
Brick houses	4	2	4	8	0	2	0	0
Wood houses	16	10	42	52	22	92	20	52
Whites								
Brick houses	208	94	222	254	26	28	12	2
Wood houses	54	128	264	204	160	228	156	266

Source: *Census of the City of Charleston*, 1861. These data were collected by sampling every other page from the printed census. The table gives the results of this sampling procedure multiplied by two.

[a]That is, slaves living with free blacks.

cases, some legislation was written early in the history of urban slavery as well as during its last decade. This legislation too was sporadically enforced, and complaints about these practices were voiced into the early 1860s.

In 1806, Charleston required that slaves who lived apart from their masters acquire written permission or tickets. Savannah had a similar law in its 1839 and subsequent legislation, as did New Orleans in its 1831 *Digest of Ordinances*.[32] Industrial Richmond had the most complex system of hiring and living out. Slaves who were hired to the various city industries were paid for their room and board rather than receiving it in kind. *The Richmond Daily Dispatch* reported in 1852 (25 October) that slaves were receiving between seventy-five cents and one dollar a week for board money, and that the city council was considering legislating against this practice. Although the tobacco manufacturers lobbied against such a bill, it was to no avail, for by 1859 Richmond had passed ordinances prohibiting the paying of slaves in lieu of board. "[I]t shall be the duty of every hirer, owner or other employer of a

slave in the city of Richmond," read the 1859 ordinance, "to provide food and lodging for such slaves upon his own premises, or
by engaging board and lodging for them with some free person . . .
except when the slave has a wife living in the city, and he stays
with her at the house of her master."[33] In 1843 a Mobile ordinance stated that slaves could live apart from their owners only
if the latter posted a bond of one hundred dollars for each grown
slave living out.[34] By 1858, however, slaves in Mobile could live
apart from their masters without the posting of bond as long as
they were properly registered.

The institution of living out provided additional flexibility which
enabled slavery to compete effectively with a free labor system in
the city. Owners, in general, desired that their slaves live apart
from them if their jobs took them to other parts of the city. The
tobacco manufacturers were against having to provide food and
lodging directly rather than by monetary payments, because, all
things considered, direct provision cost them more. Furthermore,
most accounts agree that the slaves themselves preferred the payment systems. Although whites who tried to legislate against such
practices claimed that slaves were being exploited, slaves appear
to have thought otherwise. Living out was probably tied directly
to the growth in hiring out and self-hire. It was another way in
which slavery was transformed in the cities.

Occupations and Education

Slaves were employed in an enormously varied number of positions in the cities. Although it is impossible to assess the precise
skill mixture, the cities seem to have had a higher percentage of
skilled slaves than did the rural areas. I have found only two official lists of slave skills—one for Charleston and one for Savannah,
both from 1848 city censuses. The data are given in table 11.
The Savannah list clearly undercounts slaves in skilled positions,
for it does not list occupations which slaves are known to have
held in that city. For example, the Savannah ordinances list badge
fees for caulkers, bricklayers, tailors, bakers, and carpenters, but
the census does not have either slaves or free blacks in these
categories.

Charleston's census of 1848, which appears to be more accurate than that for Savannah, reports that 17 percent of the male
slave labor force had substantial skills.[35] There were certain skilled

TABLE 11   Occupations of Adult Slaves in Charleston and Savannah, 1848

Charleston
Males and Females (Females underlined)

Occupation	Males	Females	Occupation	Males	Females
Boatmen	7		Coachmakers	3	
Coachmen	15		Confectioners	4	
Domestic servants	1,888	3,384	Cooks	3	_11_
Draymen	67		Coopers	61	
Fishermen	15		Mantua makers		_4_
Fruiterers		_1_	Mechanics (unclassified)	45	
Gardeners	3		Nurses		_2_
Hucksters		_11_	Painters	9	
Laborers (unspec.)	838	_378_	Pastry cook		_1_
Market sellers		_6_	Plasterers	16	
Porters	35		Printers	5	
Sailors	43		Saddlers	2	
Sexton	1		Seamstresses		_20_
Stevedores	2		Ship carpenters	51	
Washerwomen		_33_	Shoe makers	2	
Apprentices	43	_8_	Tailors	36	
Bakers	39		Tinners	3	
Barbers	4		Upholsterer	1	
Blacksmiths	40		Wharf builders	10	
Bookbinders	3		Subtotal	3,496	3,859
Bootmakers	4		Superannuated and disabled	38	54
Brass founder	1		Total	3,534	3,913
Bricklayers	68				
Butchers	6		**Savannah** (Males only)		
Cabinet makers	8		Mechanics	74	
Carpenters	110		Butchers	5	
Cigar makers	5		Barbers	1	
			Engineers and pilots	4	
			Total	84	

Sources: *Census of the City of Savannah*, 1848. *Census of the City of Charleston for 1848.*

Comments

The Charleston census figures are reported incorrectly in Ulrich B. Phillips, *American Negro Slavery*, p. 403. Phillips makes several errors in copying the data, omits certain occupations, and lists others which are not given.

The original Charleston and Savannah listings do not give a definition of the term "adult," but it appears as if all persons were canvassed. The Charleston census states: "The total number of male slaves between the ages of 10 and 80 were 3,724; deducting the ascertained occupations from this amount and there remains only 318 whose occupations have not been ascertained" (p. 30). In discussing the female slave data it relates that: "The total number of female slaves between the ages of 15 and 80 were 3,931; deducting the amount of ascertained occupations from this and there remain but 72 whose avocations have not been ascertained" (p. 30). The totals given in the above listing of 3,534 and 3,913 (including superannu-

TABLE 11—*Continued*

ated and disabled) are correct; the census of Charleston tabulations contain errors in addition.

The discrepancy between the total numbers of slaves in the age brackets given in the above quotation and those in the 1850 *Federal Census* appears to be due to the treatment of an area of Charleston called the "Neck." See notes to table 2 for a similar discussion concerning the white and free black data.

It does not appear that all occupations for Savannah's slaves were tabulated in this census. There were approximately 1,753 adult male slaves (over 14 years old) in Savannah in 1848. This was computed from the Savannah 1848 figure of 6,323 for all black residents from which 600 free blacks were subtracted. This was multiplied by .47 to get the number of males and then again by .65 to get the number over 14 years old.

---

trades which slaves dominated to a surprising degree. Slaves constituted 45 percent of the work force according to the occupational listing of the *Charleston Census for 1848* and were represented approximately to that degree in the building and shipping trades. About 43 percent of Charleston's carpenters were slaves, 73 percent of the coopers, 87 percent of the blacksmiths, 32 percent of the painters, and 49 percent of the ship carpenters. Free blacks were highly represented in these trades as well (see table 2). Slaves were also trained to a great extent in other trades: 43 percent of Charleston's butchers and 45 percent of the blacksmiths were slaves.

Charleston probate records for 1850 and 1860 further attest to this high level of skill. They indicate that slaves associated with the Charleston shipping trade were employed as coopers, mechanics, and engineers, while those in the housing industry were carpenters, plasterers, bricklayers, and painters. Female slaves also became semiskilled in nursing, sewing, and cooking. Since probate records do not generally list the occupation of every slave, they cannot be used to compute the percentage of slaves who had skills. But if there are no changing biases through time, one can compute how this percentage *moved* through time. The probate records for Charleston indicate that during the period 1850–60 the percentage of skilled slaves residing in that city *increased*.[36]

The mortality schedules of the 1850 and 1860 federal population censuses are another source of information about slave skills because marshals were supposed to list the occupation of each person who died during the previous year. The Norfolk mortality schedule of 1850—which is much more complete in its slave information than those for some other cities—lists slaves in positions such as barkeeper, drayman, cook, ship carpenter, cartman, carriage driver, caulker, fireman, oysterman, butcher, mariner, and blacksmith. Out of twenty-two male slaves over fifteen years of age with listed occupations, only two were listed as house servants and eight as laborers; each of the others had some trade, which points to a high level of slave skill in Norfolk. Judgment must be reserved, however, because there is no basis for assuming that those slaves without a listed occupation were not unskilled.

Slaves in many cities were apprenticed to skilled artisans. Urban newspapers had numerous advertisements enticing the owners of slaves to apprentice them to local tradesmen, such as that in the *Richmond Enquirer* (30 December 1831) announcing that James Bosher would "take as apprentices in coach smith shop six strong, active, intelligent, coloured boys, for a term not less than five years." Many slaves who were not formally apprenticed were the skilled helpers of local tradesmen. The *Charleston Courier* reported in 1832 (22 May) that "the master builder, if a bricklayer, has his own slaves; . . . the master carpenter, the same."

Slaves filled almost all positions in the local markets and stores. One New Orleans observer in 1835 remarked that, "our butchers are negroes; our fishmongers negroes, our venders of vegetables, fruit and flowers are all negroes—but what is worse, with very few exceptions the only purchasers that frequent the markets are negroes, and generally slaves" (*New Orleans Bee*, 13 October 1835). A petition to the city council of Charleston in 1826 noted that slaves were used as salesmen in stores and shops, and generally as clerks.[37]

Almost all cities used slaves on public works projects, especially in the fire department. Savannah's fire department was described by a visitor from Charleston as being "well organized . . . formed by black and colored persons, under the command of white officers" (*Charleston Courier*, 22 June 1854). Cities not only hired out but also purchased slaves for public works projects, and a few cities required that slaves living within their precincts do such duty as a mandatory service to the community.

Some cities had large numbers of slaves working in industrial pursuits. Richmond had the largest industrial slave labor force; its

tobacco factories were manned almost exclusively by slaves, and
its iron foundries had switched to slave labor by the 1850s. New
Orleans as well had slaves employed in industry; an 1836 *New
Orleans Bee* editorial (2 June) commented that "the sugar refinery
of [this city] shows that extent to which a factory may be brought
in Louisiana. The work is done chiefly by negroes."

The industrial use of slaves was not confined to the cities
however, but was widespread in the rural community. For information on rural industry, the reader is advised to consult Robert
Starobin's *Industrial Slavery in the Old South*. Recent research
using probate records has demonstrated that agricultural slaves
were also a very skilled group.[38]

The almost universal prohibition against teaching slaves to read
and write probably struck hardest in the cities, where slaves would
have been more profitable to their owners with even rudimentary
reading and writing skills. Nevertheless, many urban slaves did
acquire elementary literacy tools, possibly from their churches, or
their free friends, or the city streets with their signs and papers.
Evidence on slave literacy is sparse. Newspaper advertisement
for runaways often stated that the slave in question could read
and write, and slaves are reported to have forged passes and other
official documents. The use of tickets or passes for dock work was
ruled out as a deterrent to slaves' stealing from the Charleston
wharves because "a written permit . . . is easily obtained, not only
from white persons . . . but from slaves and free persons of color
who being able to write, readily manufacture tickets."[39]

Despite the diversity of slave occupations in some cities, the
majority of the slaves in others were house servants. Richmond,
Mobile, New Orleans, Norfolk, Savannah, and Charleston probably contained the most varied slave occupations, and Saint Louis,
Louisville, Baltimore, and Washington the least diversified.

Human capital theory—the branch of economics dealing with
investment in education and training—implies that a labor system
in which the employer can reap all returns from investments in the
employee will encourage large investments and therefore result in
high skill levels. Investments in specific skills might be expected
to increase more than other forms of training under slavery because of the higher certainty of recouping benefits.[40] More general
types of investments would also increase if the employer has

greater knowledge of returns than the employee. Further, if employers had better access to the market than their younger and poorer employees, slavery again would enable higher investment levels. This would be true, however, only if there were not a high probability that a skilled slave would run away. The finding that the American slave experience did not leave blacks a totally unskilled group is thus consistent with economic theory.

Slaves and the Law

Some aspects of the law as it related to slaves have been discussed in the previous section. What needs to be done here, however, is to indicate the extent of both serious criminal activity among urban slaves and harassment of slaves by legal authorities. This determination is crucial to the debate presented in chapter 1. I shall also consider the enforcement of these laws because only information on enforcement can indicate whether a costly burden was imposed on slaveowners. Urban slaves were bound to the same laws that affected slaves in rural areas but were also subject to a set of restrictions governing activity specific to the city, and it is with these that this section is concerned.

Stealing was reported as being especially easy for slaves in urban areas, for many of them worked in stores and on the docks. More importantly, the city afforded them a way of getting rid of pilfered goods, and illegal market operations were cheaper to operate in cities. Many of the laws governing the use of passes by slaves for the buying and selling of goods were designed to lessen the ability of slaves to get rid of stolen merchandise.

The selling of liquor to slaves was also illegal in the cities, but the practice continued, seemingly unabated. In 1855 (22 June) the *New Orleans Bee* complained about the "cabarets and drinking dens in the second and third Districts, where runaway negroes are harbored, and slaves obtain liquor in any quantity, and at all times, day and night." In 1858 (6 October) the *Daily Picayune* reported the ways New Orleans slaves escaped from the law. "A cabaret in this district . . . adjoins a negro barber saloon. The liquor sold is not drank on the premises if paid for by slaves. It is sent through by a private and secret communication into the neighboring shop, and drank there." Liquor was an issue in Louisville as well, and that city's *Daily Democrat* (17 March 1858) reported that "there are a good many groceries on Broadway where negro slaves can obtain liquor without consent of their masters. The Legislature of this State has passed a very stringent law in regard to that matter, and we hope the police of our city will enforce it." Charleston slaves went to the "Neck" to drink, and the *Courier* complained in 1845 (20 September) that the area was becoming "infested with . . . grog shops . . . [and] becoming . . . the receptacle of stolen and ill-gotten goods. . . ."

Although the urban environment afforded slaves amenities which appear to have made their bondage more tolerable, it probably also enabled them to escape more readily. Runaways from plantations flocked to the towns, where free blacks and slaves harbored them and, on occasion, helped them flee to the North. Antebellum urban newspapers were replete with advertisements which gave information concerning the occupation, abilities, and physical appearance of each escaped bondsman. A *New Orleans Daily Picayune* advertisement in 1839 (14 September) stated that runaway slave Jim Price "worked in the capacity of a butcher . . . speaks both French and English, and is very intelligent." A twenty-seven-year-old escaped slave named Garrison, according to another notice in the *Picayune* (8 December 1840), had "some knowledge of the carpenter's trade, painter's, whitewasher's, etc. and [was] no doubt employed about some of the buildings going up in the city."

In order to demonstrate the cost to urban slave users of the various slave ordinances, knowledge of enforcement is essential. Some material in the *Richmond Dispatch*, from 1852 to 1860, has provided some evidence. This newspaper listed all criminal arrests of slaves and the subsequent court hearing and sentencing. Jail fees, for example, were paid by slaveowners, generally a dollar or two for every day the slave was incarcerated. Table 12 lists those crimes of which slaves were accused in Richmond and the results of the court hearings for three years, 1852, 1854, and 1860. The absolute number of slave crimes does not appear to have increased during this period. Indeed, the *relative* number of criminal offenses decreased, because the number of slaves in Richmond increased. It is interesting to note that the single most important criminal offense in terms of the number of arrests, that of being out without a pass, was essentially dropped from the books between 1852 and 1854. The law was not changed, but the city authorities, it seems, no longer enforced it. In addition, charges of murder, many of which were witnessed, did not elicit death penalties.[41] Only in

TABLE 12   Slave Crimes in Richmond, 1852, 1854, 1860

Crimes	1852 A[a]	1852 P[b]	1854 A	1854 P	1860 A	1860 P
Out without a pass	83	41	2	0	4	2
Unlawful assembly	49	21	0	0	0	52
Runaways	36	3	18	0	0	0
Other[c]	17	128[d]	30	112[e]	24	148[f]

Source: *Richmond Dispatch* (Richmond, Virginia) 1852, 1854, 1860.
[a]Admonished or dismissed.
[b]Punished, usually with "stripes," from 5 to 39 for the worst offenses.
[c]Stealing, killing, insulting a white, trespassing, arson.
[d]Includes eight deportations and two hangings, all in instances where court found slave to have been guilty of murder or attempted murder.
[e]Two deportations, for murder or attempted murder.
[f]Six deportations, for murder or attempted murder.

one case was the death sentence handed down, in what appeared to be a premeditated and witnessed ax slaying of an entire white family. The other slaves found guilty of murder were deported to another state or to areas outside the United States. These facts do not seem to corroborate a thesis which stresses increasing costs for keeping urban slaves. Nor do they substantiate the claim that the white citizenry rid their urban areas of slaves because increasing numbers made them more troublesome.

Social aspects of slave living were also subject to control. Slaves in almost all cities could not be out at night without a pass from their owners or hirers, and passes were also required for the selling and purchasing of goods in the market. Both laws suffered from the same problems. Slaveowners found it time-consuming to write passes, and otherwise orderly slaves were caught breaking the law. The courts in many cities, after years trying cases, appear to have dropped the enforcement of these ordinances. Local merchants disagreed with them too. One grocer wrote to the *Charleston Mercury* in 1835 (6 March) that "the retailer of a yard of home-spun, or the wholesale merchant who sells a bale of cloth to a negro without a ticket, is just as liable to a prosecution for violating the law as he who sells spiritous liquors. . . . The public voice is against the law, because it is opposed by reason and justice."

Conclusion

This chapter has stressed the diversity and complexity of slavery in its urban setting. Slaves worked in more varied occupations in the cities than on the land, and a larger percentage of them were skilled. Hiring out and self-hire were common methods of employment, with living out the partner of these hiring schemes. Black neighborhoods sprang up, and slave eating and socializing centers were known in various sections of each city. In most cities, slaves were numerous enough to have carved out major sections as their domain.

Although almost every aspect of an urban slave's life was subject to the control of the master, it appears to have been more profitable to allow the slave substantial freedom of choice in living and working arrangements. As we have seen, some urban citizens tried to legislate against such freedoms, but this legislation does not seem to have greatly affected the mobility of slave labor within the city and thus its profitability as a labor force.

4   **The Apparent
        Decline of
        Urban Slavery:**
        Demographic and
        Price Data

Many of the hypotheses advanced in chapter 1 were suggested by demographic evidence showing that slave populations either declined or grew very slowly in most cities between 1850 and 1860. If one studies the census figures more closely, however, one discovers that urban slave populations went through very violent swings in their growth in the forty-year period 1820–60. Other demographic aspects of urban slavery also underwent changes during the four decades under consideration. The sex ratio, age distribution, and fertility of urban slaves changed through time and were always very different from those of their rural counterparts. The changes in these variables can best be explained by the economic model which will be developed in chapter 5. Crucial to this model is a set of slave prices and hire rates, that also display cyclical variation over time.

Changes in the Urban Slave Population, 1820–60

Table 13 presents data on the slave and free white and black populations over four decades for ten major Southern cities in absolute and in percentage rate-of-change form. The absolute figures show that the Mobile and Louisville slave populations increased between 1820 and 1850 and declined between 1850 and 1860. In other cities, such as Norfolk, Saint Louis, and Washington, slave populations oscillated, although they also displayed a decline during the last decade. Charleston had reached a peak in its slave population by 1850, and New Orleans as early as 1840. Although the city slave populations seem to follow disparate trends over these four decades, a simpler picture emerges when the data are viewed in rate-of-growth form.

Every city, with the exceptions of Mobile and New Orleans, shows a cyclical pattern in the percentage rate of change in slave populations over the four decades. The percentage increase for the

TABLE 13 Population Data for Ten Southern Cities, 1820–60

A. Slave and Free[a] Populations

Cities	1820 Slave	1820 Free	1830 Slave	1830 Free	1840 Slave	1840 Free	1850 Slave	1850 Free	1860 Slave	1860 Free
Baltimore	4357	58381	4120	76500	3199	99114	2946	166108	2218	210100
Charleston	12652	12128	15354	14935	14673	14588	19532	23453	13909	26613
Louisville	1031	2979	2406	7935	3430	17780	5432	37762	4903	63130
Mobile[b]	836	1836	1175	2019	3869	8803	6803	13712	7587	21671
New Orleans	7355	19821	9397	20340	23448	78745	17011	99364	13385	155290
Norfolk	3261	5217	3756	6058	3709	7211	4295	10031	3284	11336
Richmond	4387	7680	6345	9715	7509	12644	9927	17643	11699	26211
Saint Louis[c]	1810	8210	2796	11419	1531	14938	2656	75204	1542	159231
Savannah[d]	3075	4448	4000	4500	4694	6520	6231	9081	7712	14580
Washington	1945	11302	2330	16496	1713	21651	2113	37888	1774	59348

B. Decennial Rates of Change

	1820–30 Slave	1820–30 Free	1830–40 Slave	1830–40 Free	1840–50 Slave	1840–50 Free	1850–60 Slave	1850–60 Free
Baltimore	-5%	31%	-22%	30%	-8%	68%	-25%	26%
Charleston	21	23	-4	-2	33	61	-29	13
Louisville	133	166	43	124	58	112	-10	67
Mobile	41	10	229	336	76	56	12	58
New Orleans	28	3	150	287	-27	26	-21	56
Norfolk	15	16	-1	19	16	39	-24	13
Richmond	45	26	18	30	32	40	18	49
Saint Louis	54	39	-45	31	73	403	-42	112
Savannah	30	0	17	44	33	39	24	61

	1820 White	1820 Black	1830 White	1830 Black	1840 White	1840 Black	1850 White	1850 Black	1860 White	1860 Black
Baltimore	48055	10326	61710	14790	81147	17967	140666	25442	184520	25680
Charleston	10653	1475	12828	2107	13030	1558	20012	3441	23376	3237
Louisville	2886	93	7703	232	17161	619	36224	1538	61213	1917
Mobile[b]	1653	183	1647	372	8262	541	12997	715	20854	817
New Orleans	13584	6237	12299	8041	59519	19226	89459	9905	144601	10689
Norfolk	4618	599	5130	928	6185	1026	9075	956	10290	1046
Richmond	6445	1235	7755	1960	10718	1926	15274	2369	23635	2576
Saint Louis[c]	8014	196	11109	220	14407	531	73806	1398	157476	1755
Savannah[d]	3866	582	4048	452	5888	632	8395	686	13875	705
Washington	9606	1696	13367	3129	16843	4808	29730	8158	50139	9209

Source: *Federal Population Census*, 1860, 1850, 1840, 1830, and 1820.

[a] Free white as well as free black.

[b] 1820 Mobile returns are for Mobile County.

[c] 1820 and 1830 Saint Louis returns are for Saint Louis County.

[d] No Census population data were given for Savannah in 1830. The 1830 slave and free figures are approximations based on the manuscript census figures.

decades 1820–30 and 1840–50 is greater (and the decrease, in the case of Baltimore, is correspondingly smaller), than for the other two decades. In addition, the swings of these cycles are very large. Many cities experienced huge increases in slaves during the first and third decades and decreases during the other two decades. The free black population also experienced a dampened rate of growth in the last decade. Some cities—for example, Richmond —experienced increases in their slave populations throughout the forty-year period, but the increases were still cyclical in rate-of-change form. Therefore, a theory which attempts to explain why urban slavery declined in its last decade must be consistent with the large oscillations in the growth of the urban slave population during the entire period.

The ten cities listed in table 13 were the largest Southern cities for which population statistics could be collected over the whole period 1820–60. Statistics for all twelve cities listed in table 14, whose total populations exceeded five thousand in 1860, could be collected only for 1850 and 1860. The figures suggest that little is gained by expanding the sample, although the additional data serve to mitigate the 1850–60 decline in the urban slave population. More importantly, since cities other than the ten listed in table 13 were very small prior to 1850, no serious bias is expected from using the data in that table.

Because data on the slave labor force, as opposed to mere population data, are not available, I have had to take, as a proxy for the labor force, slaves who were of working age. The five censuses for 1820–60 give age breakdowns for slaves, but the age limits reported are not comparable among all decades. The censuses for 1830 and 1840 had different age brackets than those for 1850 and 1860, and the age breakdowns for 1820 were extremely broad and not very useful. Computation of the labor force figures in terms of the percentage of the slave population between ten and fifty-four years of age required a reformulation of the data, which is presented in table 15. The 1850 and 1860 statistics have here been expressed in terms of the 1830 and 1840 age categories. These numbers were calculated by sampling about one-eighth of the reported slave population data in the 1850 and 1860 census manuscripts. The 1820, 1830, and 1840 data could not be transformed into the narrower, and therefore more useful, 1850 and

TABLE 14   Slave Population Data for Twelve Southern Cities, 1850 and 1860

City	1850	1860
Augusta, Georgia	4718	3663
Alexandria, Virginia	1061	1386
Fredericksburg, Virginia	1174	1291
Lynchburg, Virginia	3424	2694
Memphis, Tennessee	2360	3684
Montgomery, Alabama	2119	4400
Nashville, Tennessee	2028	3226
Natchez, Mississippi	3031	2138
New Bern, North Carolina	1927	2383
Portsmouth, Virginia	1751	934
Petersburg, Virginia	4729	5680
Wilmington, North Carolina	3031	3777
Aggregate Urban Slave Population, 1850 and 1860		
10 Cities (listed in table 13)	76,900	68,000
22 Cities (listed in tables 13 and 14)	108,275	104,228
Decennial Rate of Change, 1850-60		
10 Cities (listed in table 13)		-12%
22 Cities (listed in tables 13 and 14)		-4%

Source: *Federal Population Census*, 1850 and 1860.

1860 age brackets, because the former data are not available by individuals in the original manuscripts.

The labor force percentages were used to compute the average annual rate of change[1] for the slave labor force given in table 16. The labor force figures show oscillations in some cases more extreme and in others somewhat less than those in the population data (also shown in table 16). Although these statistics, being derived from age distribution data, are subject to sampling error, they will be used in chapter 5 in estimating important demand

TABLE 15 Age Distributions for Ten City Slave Populations and Total United States Slave Population

Percentage of Male (Female) Slave Population in Various Age Categories

Year and Age	Balti-more	Charles-ton	Louis-ville	Mobile	New Orleans	Norfolk	Rich-mond	Saint Louis	Savannah[a]	Washing-ton	Total U.S.
1830											
0-9	27(19)	31(27)	25(23)	22(28)	31(22)	32(26)	22(24)	31(31)	25(24)	30(24)	35
10-23	41(46)	30(27)	30(37)	34(31)	29(31)	28(29)	33(31)	37(36)	29(29)	37(38)	31
24-35	20(21)	22(24)	31(26)	29(27)	24(31)	19(20)	25(21)	21(20)	21(23)	19(20)	18
36-54	10(11)	13(15)	12(12)	14(11)	11(12)	16(17)	15(18)	8(11)	19(18)	11(13)	12
> 54	3(4)	4(7)	2(3)	2(3)	4(4)	6(8)	5(7)	3(2)	6(5)	3(5)	4
1840											
0-9	24(18)	30(25)	29(24)	20(22)	24(20)	34(21)	17(20)	25(24)	24(23)	29(22)	34
10-23	43(47)	29(28)	34(40)	31(33)	27(30)	26(24)	33(34)	40(43)	31(31)	42(41)	31
24-35	20(22)	25(28)	20(20)	34(29)	32(34)	21(21)	30(20)	24(19)	22(22)	15(18)	19
36-54	10(10)	13(15)	15(13)	11(12)	14(13)	12(24)	16(19)	10(12)	17(20)	10(14)	12
> 54	3(3)	4(4)	3(3)	4(4)	4(3)	7(10)	3(6)	2(3)	5(5)	3(5)	4
1850											
0-9	22(16)	20(17)	26(22)	20(24)	26(16)	26(21)	15(20)	22(19)	21(23)	28(21)	32
10-23	51(48)	31(27)	37(39)	25(29)	30(28)	31(35)	36(34)	33(36)	36(34)	41(41)	
24-35	15(19)	21(21)	20(20)	31(23)	27(29)	23(16)	25(20)	29(26)	20(22)	17(18)	
36-54	10(13)	19(23)	14(16)	20(18)	13(22)	15(20)	19(18)	13(16)	18(18)	11(13)	
> 54	2(4)	9(12)	3(3)	4(6)	4(5)	5(8)	4(8)	3(3)	4(4)	3(7)	(5)[b]
1860											
0-9	21(16)	20(20)	25(21)	23(21)	19(15)	25(17)	13(21)	28(20)	23(21)	30(14)	31
10-23	46(41)	29(29)	37(35)	25(29)	30(30)	34(33)	40(32)	33(39)	31(29)	38(40)	
24-35	20(22)	23(20)	19(20)	26(25)	28(27)	17(17)	27(21)	18(19)	20(18)	15(19)	

1830	.75	.66	.74	.73	.71	.64	.71	.67	.73	.69	.61
1840	.77	.69	.71	.75	.75	.65	.77	.73	.72	.71	.62
1850	.79	.71	.73	.73	.75	.70	.76	.77	.74	.71	.64
1860	.76	.72	.72	.72	.79	.70	.79	.71	.70	.72	.64

Sources: *Federal Population Census*, 1830, 1840, 1850, and 1860; *Federal Population Census*, manuscript slave schedules, 1850 and 1860.

[a]1850 figures are for Chatham County.

[b]This figure is for female slaves and has been computed on the assumption that 60 percent of females aged fifty to fifty-nine were between fifty and fifty-four.

[c]Approximations based on the *Federal Population Census*, 1820.

TABLE 16   Average Annual Rates of Change in Slave Populations and Labor Forces for Ten Cities, Three Urban Aggregates, and the Total United States

Cities and Aggregates	Slave Population				Slave Labor Force			
	1820-30	1830-40	1840-50	1850-60	1820-30	1830-40	1840-50	1850-60
Baltimore	-.006	-.025	-.008	-.028	.004	-.023	-.006	-.032
Charleston	.019	-.005	.029	-.034	.018	.000	.031	-.033
Louisville	.085	.035	.046	-.010	.098	.031	.049	-.012
Mobile	.034	.119	.056	.011	.037	.122	.054	.010
New Orleans	.025	.091	-.032	-.024	.015	.097	-.032	-.019
Norfolk	.014	-.001	.015	-.027	.014	.000	.022	-.027
Richmond	.037	.017	.028	.016	.044	.025	.026	.020
Saint Louis	.043	-.060	.055	-.054	.045	-.052	.060	-.062
Savannah	.026	.016	.028	.021	.032	.013	.032	.016
Washington	.018	-.031	.021	-.017	.026	-.028	.021	-.016
Old South Cities[a]	.023	.004	.027	-.009	.025	.008	.029	-.007
New South Cities[b]	.026	.095	-.014	-.013	.017	.100	-.014	-.010
Border State Cities[c]	.024	-.017	.029	-.023	.032	-.014	.031	-.026
Total U.S. Rural and Urban	.027	.021	.025	.021	.025	.023	.029	.021

Sources: Tables 13 and 14. Although certain cities underwent boundary changes during the period studied, most of these extensions do not affect the conclusions about the slave population cycles. A few cities grew by annexing nearby towns during those decades when the aggregate slave population declined or grew more slowly than previously.

[a]Charleston, Norfolk, Richmond, and Savannah.

[b]Mobile and New Orleans.

[c]Baltimore, Louisville, Saint Louis, and Washington.

parameters. Data on the average annual rate of change for urban free populations, given in table 17, will also be used in chapter 5 in estimating the model.[2]

Table 15 shows how the age composition of the urban slave population differed from that of the total (rural and urban) slave population and how both changed through time. The most interesting characteristics of the urban slave population concern the two tails of the age distribution. Whereas the percentage of children was smaller in the city, the percentage of older slaves, especially older women, was much larger.

The 1830 and 1840 urban percentages for older slaves are not much different from the total U.S. figures. Some cities, for example Norfolk and Richmond, had a slightly older female slave labor force than the other cities, but this older age bracket does not

TABLE 17   Average Annual Rates of Change in Free Populations
for Ten Cities and Three Urban Aggregates

Cities and Aggregates	Free Population			
	1820-30	1830-40	1840-50	1850-60
Baltimore	.027	.026	.052	.023
Charleston	.021	-.002	.047	.013
Louisville	.098	.081	.075	.051
Mobile	.010	.147	.044	.046
New Orleans	.003	.135	.023	.045
Norfolk	.015	.017	.033	.012
Richmond	.024	.026	.033	.040
Saint Louis	.033	.027	.162	.075
Savannah	.001	.037	.033	.047
Washington	.038	.027	.056	.045
Old South Cities[a]	.018	.015	.038	.027
New South Cities[b]	.003	.136	.026	.045
Border State Cities[c]	.033	.031	.073	.044

[a]Charleston, Norfolk, Richmond, and Savannah.
[b]Mobile and New Orleans.
[c]Baltimore, Louisville, Saint Louis, and Washington.

show an abnormal bulge before 1840. This had changed some-what by 1850 and differences had become striking by 1860. At that time all cities except New Orleans had a greater percentage of females older than 54 years than did the United States in general. In some cities, for example, Norfolk and Washington, the percentage was double that for the United States. The cities which showed the greatest change in this statistic between 1850 and 1860 were Baltimore, Louisville, Norfolk, Saint Louis, Savannah, and Washington. Four of these cities—Baltimore, Louisville, Saint Louis, and Washington—had slave populations which underwent other extreme changes during this period. The fact that they were border-state cities will be shown to have much to do with these dramatic shifts.

One explanation for these changes is that during the period when slaves were being sold and hired from the city, those with specific skills were retained. Domestic skills, depending largely on experience, are probably highly specific to an individual household. Furthermore, personal attachments between family members and domestic help are formed and can also be considered as specific skills. It is likely, therefore, that between 1850 and 1860, when prices for slaves in the rural South were rising, younger rather than older females were sold or hired out from the city.

As to children, not only was the percentage of the slave population under ten years old smaller in the cities than in the rural areas for the entire period under study, but it was strikingly so by 1860. Part of this phenomenon is related to the demographic change described above: as the urban female population became older, a smaller proportion of the women were of childbearing age. Fertility data presented in table 18, however, which express children per thousand women between fifteen and forty-four years of age, show this to be an insufficient explanation.

The fertility ratios were substantially lower in the cities than in the rural areas.[3] Part of the difference is due to the lower fertility of all urban women, without regard to color or free status. The statistics for free blacks and whites in the cities demonstrate this point. But the urban fertility ratios are lowest of all for slaves. Although some children under ten might have been boarded out by their owners on plantations and thus would not appear in urban census figures, the data still point to a lower number of *births* in cities.

TABLE 18   Fertility Ratios for Ten Cities and Two States

City (County) or State and Year	Slave[a]	Free Black[b]	Free White[b]
Part A: Children under one year per thousand women 15-44 years of age.			
Baltimore (Baltimore)			
1860	36	78 (100.0%)	121 (100.0%)
1850	22	94 (87.5)	125 (80.4)
Charleston (Charleston)			
1860	55	85 (89.3)	98 (81.4)
1850	42	42 (89.3)	64 (80.2)
Louisville (Jefferson)			
1860	81	44 (79.4)	92 (95.5)
1850	72	129 (76.6)	86 (93.9)
Mobile (Mobile)			
1850	91	139 (68.3)	111 (73.0)
1860	63	65 (75.9)	136 (75.1)
New Orleans (Orleans)			
1860	40	40 (97.7)	86 (97.8)
1850	50	86 (99.4)	105 (97.0)
Norfolk (Norfolk)			
1860	42	99 (37.3)	122 (42.2)
1850	54	82 (41.4)	88 (44.6)
Richmond (Henrico)			
1860	75	92 (71.8)	137 (62.3)
1850	46	81 (65.1)	87 (64.1)
Saint Louis (Saint Louis)			
1860	71	67 (94.1)	158 (85.4)
1850	43	71 (98.3)	117 (87.3)
Savannah (Chatham)			
1860	82	82 (97.2)	119 (89.4)
1850	80[c]	93 (93.8)	89 (91.7)
Washington (Washington)			
1860	54	91 (82.7)	128 (82.5)
1850	68	87 (81.1)	101 (78.4)
Virginia			
1860	136	120	135
1850	116	110	120
Louisiana			
1860	103	60	117
1850	82	84	122

TABLE 18—*Continued*

City or State and Year	Slave	Free Black	Free White
Part B: Children under 4 years per thousand women 15-44 years of age[d].			
Baltimore			
1860	176	343	568
1850	181	433	575
Charleston			
1860	352	471	518
1850	402	408	478
Louisville			
1860	345	452	809
1850	366	429	610
Mobile			
1860	423	588	577
1850	485	531	611
New Orleans			
1860	270	364	527
1850	271	371	447
Norfolk			
1860	393	514	553
1850	373	513	513
Richmond			
1860	393	447	597
1850	368	440	537
Saint Louis			
1860	351	331	662
1850	328	338	542
Savannah			
1860	448	533	543
1850	442[c]	520	490
Washington			
1860	255	419	548
1850	338	433	521
Virginia			
1860	769	639	705
1850	791	631	686
Louisiana			
1860	575	448	672
1850	562	466	656

Sources: *Federal Population Census*, 1860 and 1850; *Federal Population Census*, manuscript slave schedules, 1860 and 1850.

[a]These data were derived for the cities from sampling the manuscript censuses. Those for the states were computed by the method described in footnote b.

[b]Both the free black and free white data were taken from the published census volumes and therefore refer to county figures, except that for Baltimore 1860, which is for the city. The numbers in parentheses are the percentage of free whites or blacks in the county who resided in the city Most of these are high. That for Norfolk is small because the city of Ports-

TABLE 18—*Continued*

mouth is also part of Norfolk county. In constructing the number of females 15–44 years old, I assumed that 60 percent of those 40–50 were 40–44 years old.

cThis number refers to Chatham County because the Savannah 1850 data are not available. Fifty-two percent of Chatham County slaves were located in Savannah.

dThe percentages in parentheses from part A apply here but have not been repeated.

Comments

The fertility ratios for children under one year per thousand women 15–45 show extreme changes from 1850 to 1860. Mobile, Richmond, and Saint Louis appear to have strikingly more fertile women slaves in 1860 than in 1850. This observation also holds for Virginia and Louisiana slaves. Free urban white fertility also rises for seven of the ten cities from 1850 to 1860. It appears that this may not reflect any real trends but may be the product of errors in the census data. The percentage of slaves 0–5 in 1850 who lived to be 10–15 in 1860 is over 100. This implies that there were either too few slaves 0–5 in 1850 or too many counted in the 10–15 age group in 1860. The former hypothesis is consistent with the observation that fertility ratios rose from 1850 to 1860. That ratio which uses children 0–5 does not vary as much over time, and therefore it is most probable that children 0–1 were undercounted in the 1850 census.

The nature of urban employment may explain fertility ratios and age distributions. Urban work was generally less structured than was agricultural labor, and therefore demanded more mobility. Hiring out and self-hire were widespread and appear to have increased over time. Although table 9 shows that children were hired out with their parents, a young child was still a net loss to the hirer. Employers wanted compensation for hiring very young slaves, and so they paid owners less for a mother and child together than for the mother alone.[4] Children were therefore less desired in the cities, where there was much slave hiring, than on plantations, where they might be looked after in large groups. Female slaves who were infertile, unmarried, or childless for any reason would command a premium in the cities relative to the rural areas.[5]

One must also consider that there were more female slaves than males in the cities and that fertility would be low if spouses were infrequently visited. When the data are expressed as children per thousand *male* slaves between fifteen and forty-four years of age, the resulting fertility ratios bear more resemblance to those of free blacks and whites in the cities.

The possibility that some youngsters were kept on plantations does not necessarily imply that families were broken, for periods of hire in the cities were rarely longer than one year, and many plantations were close by. Table 19 gives the female-to-male ratios for slaves in various age classifications. In all but two cases, the female-to-male ratio for children is greater than 1.00, and in four cases it exceeds 1.25. Although this suggests that urban masters may have kept the *male* children of their urban slaves on plantations, it can also be explained along previous lines. Mothers with female children were probably worth more in the cities than in the rural areas and should, therefore, have been found in greater abundance there. Female children may have been more valuable than were males in the cities, because of the training in domestic skills they gained by working with their mothers. Newspaper accounts of the period often referred to female slave children as taking care of the babies of their white owners. Therefore it seems possible that slaveowners and hirers took advantage of the mobility of the slave labor force to seek out urban employment for women who, if not childless, had only female children.

TABLE 19   Female-to-Male Ratios for Slaves, by Age, for Ten Cities, 1860

City	Aged 0-9	Aged 10-23	Aged 24-35	Aged 36-54	Aged >54
Baltimore	1.75	2.05	2.53	3.58	4.03
Charleston	1.10	1.10	0.96	1.15	1.41
Louisville	1.26	1.42	1.58	1.80	2.63
Mobile	0.91	1.16	0.96	0.95	1.00
New Orleans	1.18	1.50	1.45	1.82	1.50
Norfolk	1.02	1.46	1.50	1.67	3.25
Richmond	1.29	0.51	0.62	1.00	1.20
Saint Louis	1.29	2.13	1.90	1.92	1.80
Savannah	1.04	1.07	1.03	1.46	1.28
Washington	0.98	2.21	2.66	3.57	3.00

Source: Tables 1 and 15.

The cities contained a greater percentage of female slaves of all ages than did rural areas, and many cities, especially those in the border states, experienced an increase in this percentage over time. Table 20 shows that, by 1860, there were at least three females for every two male slaves in six of the ten cities listed, and two-thirds of the slave populations of Baltimore, Louisville, Saint Louis, and Washington were females. Because there were large increases in this ratio between 1850 and 1860, the outflow of slaves from Border State cities during this decade was largely male. This again can be explained within the context of a selective migration. Those slaves whose marginal products† were higher in the cities than in the rural areas—possibly because of specific training—were kept in the cities. The others became part of the Southern agricultural labor force.

The decline in the urban slave population and the change in its composition during the 1850s were merely part of a larger phenomenon. The number of rural slaves varied similarly over this period, and although the cycles were smaller than those experienced in the cities, they were large enough to create wide changes in the prices of slaves.

Table 21 shows the aggregate slave figures for the United States and the decennial rates of growth for four decades. The rates of growth are greater for the first and third than for the second and fourth decades. These fluctuations have been attributed to the "echo effects" of the increased importation of mature blacks prior to the embargo placed on slave importations.[6] In other words, there was a large increase in the slave population one generation after the embargo, as the children of the last group of African arrivals reached childbearing age.

Data concerning the bulge in the importation of adult slaves just before the embargo must come from indirect estimates, because the censuses from 1790 to 1810 did not report age and sex breakdowns. DuBois states that "between 1803 to 1807, 39,075 Negroes were imported into Charleston," but adds that "it is, of course, highly probable that the Custom House returns were much below the actual figures."[7]

---

†The marginal product of a laborer is the increase in quantity produced from adding one more worker, holding other factors constant. It is usually defined as the change in total product divided by the change in the number of inputs.

TABLE 20   Female-to-Male Ratios for Slaves and Whites, for Ten Cities, 1820–60

City	1820		1830		1840		1850		1860	
	Slave	White	Slave	White	Slave	White	Slave	White	Slave	White
Baltimore	1.21	1.01	1.48	1.05	1.74	1.09	2.11	0.98	2.28	1.08
Charleston	1.22	1.00	1.26	1.03	1.32	0.91	1.26	0.95	1.12	1.00
Louisville	1.08	0.58	1.12	0.59	1.48	0.85	1.25	0.86	1.49	0.96
Mobile	0.86	0.50	0.92	0.51	1.04	0.46	1.12	0.85	0.96	0.81
New Orleans	1.72	0.64	1.79	0.67	1.39	0.71	1.50	0.73	1.49	0.92
Norfolk	1.24	1.11	1.38	1.07	1.48	1.14	1.56	1.16	1.48	1.11
Richmond	1.02	0.85	0.95	0.95	0.90	0.97	0.87	0.96	0.76	0.91
Saint Louis	0.83	0.66	1.05	0.73	1.20	0.63	1.10	0.74	1.77	0.89
Savannah	1.32	0.84	1.35	0.92	1.37	0.82	1.11	0.90	1.14	0.83
Washington	1.21	1.01	1.28	1.03	1.64	1.06	1.88	1.05	2.09	1.06

Source: *Federal Population Census*, 1820, 1830, 1840, 1850, and 1860.

TABLE 21   United States Total Slave Population and Decennial
Rates of Growth, 1820–60

A.	Total Slave Population (to nearest thousand)	
	1820	1,538,000
	1830	2,009,000
	1840	2,487,000
	1850	3,205,000
	1860	3,954,000
B.	Decennial Rates of Growth	
	1820-30	30.6
	1830-40	23.8
	1840-50	28.8
	1850-60	23.4

Source: *Federal Population Census*, 1820, 1830, 1840, 1850, and 1860.

If one accepts the figure of 39,075 slaves imported during this period, the implied rate of natural increase would be greater than during any other decade of American slavery. This is highly unlikely, especially for that particular decade. During that period the percentage of slaves who were newly arrived Africans was quite substantial, and recent imports were more susceptible to disease than were the American-born stock. If one assumes a more realistic rate of increase, similar to that for the decades just after the embargo, a figure of 90,000 imported slaves results. This is, in fact, a lower-bound estimate, because the survivor rate was probably smaller during this decade than during the later ones. Using a more reasonable survivor rate for the entire population yields approximately 100,000 imported slaves for the period 1800 to 1807.[8]

One way of making inferences about the nature of imports during this period is by observing the price ratio of female to male slaves from the 1790s to 1807. One would expect this ratio to have declined during the pre-embargo period, because a large number of female slaves of childbearing age were probably brought into the United States just before the embargo. Table 22 shows some evidence of this trend in prices. Although certainly not conclusive, these data suggest that relatively more females than males were brought into the U.S. during the period immediately preceding the embargo than were brought in during the 1790s.

TABLE 22   Ratios of Female-to-Male Slave Prices, Ann Arundel, Maryland, 1796–1810

1796	.72 (56, 76)	1804	.50 (21, 31)
1797	.70 (27, 59)	1805	.41 (24, 21)
1798	.46 (36, 40)	1806	.49 (12, 13)
1799	.71 (33, 71)	1807	.26 (9, 20)
1800	.52 (23, 20)	1808	.60 (34, 35)
1801	.54 (40, 40)	1809	.49 (25, 32)
1802	.67 (39, 40)	1810	.54 (20, 28)
1803	.51 (34, 40)		

Source: Probate Records, Slave Sales and Inventories, Ann Arundel, Maryland (Genealogical Society Microfilm, Salt Lake City, Utah).

Numbers of observations are in brackets—first, the number underlying the average female price, and second, that underlying the average male price.

The decreases in the growth rate of the slave population for the decades 1830–40 and 1850–60 may also have been partially due to cholera and yellow fever epidemics. One large outbreak began in about 1832 and took its greatest toll during the mid 1830s. Another epidemic struck Louisiana in the early 1850s and spread rapidly to other Southern states.[9]

All available evidence suggests, then, that the changes in the total slave population from 1820 to 1860 were brought about by exogenous forces. An increase in the imports of slaves just prior to the embargo, and the probability that these imports were composed of relatively more female than male slaves, serve to substantiate the theory that the small cycles in slave supply were due to "echo effects." Serious epidemics in some parts of the South strengthened these changes.

The Course of Slave Prices and Hire Rates

Until Fogel and Engerman compiled slave price and hire rate data for their study, and I did so for mine, few complete sources were available. Ulrich B. Phillips compiled price data for prime field hands in four trading areas over the period 1795–1860.[10] These statistics have recently come into question in the light of the more complete Fogel-Engerman sample, which points to upward biases in Phillips's data. It appears that Phillips's sampling techniques are the source of significant differences in peak prices between his and the Fogel-Engerman data. The only substantial compilation of hire rates has been Robert Evans's study.[11] His data also differ somewhat from those of the larger Fogel-Engerman sample because of his heavy reliance on railroad hires during certain periods. These hire rates would be expected to be above average because of risks assumed by an owner who hired his slave to a railroad company.

The data used in the present study are both those that Fogel and Engerman collected for rural areas and those that I collected for cities. These prices stem from both appraisals and sales, contained in probate records and bills of sale. Although the sale prices are about 20 percent higher than the appraised data, probably due to the incentives of the inheritance tax,[12] these differences in level do not seriously affect the trends over time, given in table 23. In fact, the two series look quite similar in rate-of-change form. Where possible, the data are also given for slaves in the labor force, defined as slaves between ten and fifty-five years of age.

The hire rate data are from guardianship accounts and are expressed as an annual rate even if the hire had been contracted for a shorter duration. Urban hire rate data are for slaves who worked in the cities. The urban prices are for slaves whose owners resided in the cities, so that the great majority of these prices are for slaves who worked in the city. The other data are by state and refer to all slaves in the state, mainly agricultural workers.

Table 24 gives the raw price and hire rate data, with the number of observations from which these mean values were obtained. All prices are expressed as a three-year moving average to smooth random fluctuations: for example, the 1850 price includes prices

TABLE 23 Average Annual Rates of Change in Slave Prices and Slave Hire Rates

A. PRICE DATA

1. Rural Appraised Prices - All Slaves

(a) Undeflated

	Georgia	Louisiana	Maryland	North Carolina	South Carolina	Virginia
1820-30	-.0483	-.0261	-.0292	n.a.	-.0403	-.0605
1830-40	.0613	.0277	.0650	.0481	.0383	.0608
1840-50	-.0002	-.0212	.0132	.0000	.0337	.0073
1850-60	.0400	.0717	n.a.	.0622	.0577	.0555

(b) Deflated[a]

	Georgia	Louisiana	Maryland	North Carolina	South Carolina	Virginia
1820-30	-.0189	.0064	.0002	n.a.	-.0109	-.0311
1830-40	.0601	.0221	.0638	.0469	.0371	.0595
1840-50	-.0049	-.0335	.0085	-.0047	.0290	.0026
1850-60	.0323	.0698	n.a.	.0545	.0500	.0477

2. Rural Appraised Prices - Labor Force[b]

	Undeflated				Deflated			
	Georgia	Louisiana	Maryland	Virginia	Georgia	Louisiana	Maryland	Virginia
1820-30	-.0455	-.0296	-.0261	n.a.	-.0161	.0029	.0033	n.a.
1830-40	.0477	.0341	.0625	.0684	.0465	.0284	.0613	.0672
1840-50	.0126	-.0160	.0063	.0089	.0079	-.0284	.0016	.0042
1850-60	.0377	.0649	n.a.	.0567	.0300	.0630	n.a.	.0490

3. Rural Sale Prices - All Slaves

	Undeflated				Deflated			
	Louisiana	N. Carolina	S. Carolina	Virginia	Louisiana	N. Carolina	S. Carolina	Virginia
1820-30	n.a.	-.0404	n.a.	n.a.	n.a.	-.0111	n.a.	n.a.
1830-40	n.a.	.0402	.0551	n.a.	n.a.	.0148	.0539	n.a.
1840-50	-.0599	.0012	.0122	-.0723	-.0723	-.0351	.0074	-.0540
1850-60	.0640	.0624	.0661	.0618	.0621	.0547	.0583	-.0119

4. City Appraised Price Data - All Slaves

	Undeflated				Deflated[c]			
	Charleston	New Orleans	Savannah	Virginia Cities[d]	Charleston	New Orleans	Savannah	Virginia Cities[d]

B. HIRE RATE DATA

1. Rural and Urban - Undeflated

	Georgia	Maryland	North Carolina	Tennessee	Virginia	Virginia Cities[d]
1820-30	n.a.	-.0234	n.a.	n.a.	-.0294	-.0047
1830-40	n.a.	.0274	.0959	n.a.	.0026	.0174
1840-50	.0159	.0182	-.0511	-.0166	.0121	-.0105
1850-60	.0784	n.a.	.0747	.0470	.0375	.0788

2. Rural and Urban - Deflated[e]

	Georgia	Maryland	North Carolina	Tennessee	Virginia	Virginia Cities[d]
1820-30	n.a.	.0060	n.a.	n.a.	.0000	.0247
1830-40	n.a.	.0262	.0947	n.a.	.0014	.0162
1840-50	.0112	.0135	-.0558	-.0213	.0074	-.0152
1850-60	.0707	n.a.	.0670	.0393	.0298	.0711

Sources: Probate Records, Slave Bills of Sale, and Guardianship Accounts (Genealogical Society, Salt Lake City, Utah); *Historical Statistics of the United States*, pp. 120 and 122. Probate records are inventories of estates which are in probate due to the death of an owner. Slaves, as well as all other property, were appraised by three separate appraisers to determine the value of the estate if the will had divided property among heirs or if there were outstanding debts. The hire rate figures come from guardianship accounts, which are records of estates left in trust for children. Slaves, in many instances, were hired out to support minors who were heirs. See table 24 for raw price and hire rate data and the price indices used.

[a] All state data are deflated by Taylor's wholesale price index for Charleston (*Historical Statistics*, p. 120), except Louisiana's, which are deflated by Taylor's wholesale price index for New Orleans (*Historical Statistics*, p. 22).

[b] Computed using prices for labor-force-age slaves, i.e., those 10–55 years.

[c] All city data are deflated by Taylor's wholesale price index for Charleston, except New Orleans, which are deflated by Taylor's wholesale price index for New Orleans.

[d] Virginia cities refer to data for Richmond, Lynchburg, and Fredericksburg for 1830 to 1860 and Richmond alone for 1820.

[e] All hire rates are deflated by Taylor's wholesale price index for Charleston.

n.a. = Not available

TABLE 24   Slave Prices, Slave Hire Rates, and Price Indices for Urban and Rural Areas, 1820–60

A. PRICES

1. Rural[a] Appraised Prices – All Slaves

	Georgia	Louisiana	Maryland	North Carolina	South Carolina	Virginia
1820	402 (169)[b]	593 (559)	174 (1100)	n.a.	359 (140)	370 (13)
1830	248 (39)	457 (315)	130 (609)	254 (344)	240 (60)	202 (153)
1840	458 (325)	603 (1454)	249 (760)	411 (505)	352 (776)	371 (1159)
1850	457 (773)	488 (2269)	284 (472)	409 (917)	493 (174)	399 (1090)
1860	682 (385)	1000 (2166)	n.a.	762 (626)	876 (224)	695 (658)

2. Rural Appraised Prices – Labor Force

	Georgia	Louisiana	Maryland	North Carolina	South Carolina	Virginia
1820	487 (77)	652 (485)	235 (671)	n.a.	469 (95)	n.a.
1830	309 (18)	485 (286)	181 (369)	n.a.	n.a.	218 (75)
1840	498 (136)	682 (1091)	338 (467)	526 (35)	363 (54)	432 (182)
1850	565 (373)	581 (1713)	360 (279)	545 (77)	572 (138)	472 (162)
1860	824 (257)	1112 (1821)	n.a.	862 (182)	n.a.	832 (136)

3. Rural Sale Prices – All Slaves

	Georgia	Louisiana	Maryland	North Carolina	South Carolina	Virginia
1820	n.a.	n.a.	n.a.	n.a.	499 (98)	n.a.
1830	n.a.	n.a.	n.a.	223 (60)	333 (94)	n.a.
1840	n.a.	825 (142)	357 (83)	387 (175)	498 (184)	459 (45)
1850	598 (49)	777 (339)	n.a.	437 (272)	504 (97)	427 (81)
1860	1200 (32)	1474 (76)	n.a.	846 (113)	941 (127)	792 (42)

4. Urban Appraised Prices

	Charleston			New Orleans			Savannah			Virginia Cities[e]		
	Males	Total	Females	Males	Total	Females	Males	Total	Females	Males	Total	Females
1820	481(193)[c]	445	409(194)[c]	750(26)[c]	798	843(28)[c]	474(17)[c]	451	435(25)[c]	308 (62)[c]	305	301 (55)[c]
	503(180)[d]	454	389(134)[d]	792(24)[d]	775	753(18)[d]	n.a.	n.a.	n.a.	339 (54)[d]	331	320 (37)[d]
1830	302 (37)	282	257 (29)	457(66)	444	433(72)	371 (7)	321	300(17)	305 (97)	275	232 (69)
	309 (36)	279	235 (24)	486(60)	450	411(54)	371 (7)	339	318(11)	319 (90)	285	227 (54)
1840	412 (91)	400	388 (93)	699(47)	646	613(76)	n.a.	n.a.	n.a.	458(111)	429	402(122)
	418 (89)	381	338 (77)	764(42)	671	604(59)	n.a.	n.a.	n.a.	501 (95)	443	388 (99)
1850	462(109)	384	304(107)	477(23)	454	439(36)	472(26)	466	461(35)	458(177)	434	392(102)
	483(103)	377	319(187)	540(20)	507	484(28)	486(24)	432	378(24)	491(158)	455	378 (73)

					Mississippi	...th Carolina	Tennessee	Virginia
1820	n.a.	n.a.	24(127)	n.a.	n.a.	n.a.	n.a.	51(52)
1830	n.a.	n.a.	19(76)	n.a.	23(372)	n.a.	n.a.	38(16)
1840	58(44)	n.a.	25(265)	54(5)	60(423)	59(612)	39(431)	
1850	68(142)	72(31)	30(179)	75(33)	36(828)	50(1110)	44(370)	
1860	149(39)	139(21)	n.a.	80(673)	76(301)	80(145)	64(179)	

2. Urban

	Virginia Cities		
	Males	Total	Females
1820	63(7)[c]	44	29(9)[c]
	68(5)[d]	44	29(8)[d]
1830	52(89)	42	18(35)
	42(72)	44	21(24)
1840	77(20)	50	30(27)
	87(16)	51	30(27)
1850	52(40)	45	28(16)
	53(39)	48	32(12)
1860	123(92)	99	52(46)
	126(88)	102	53(43)

C. TAYLOR'S WHOLESALE PRICE INDICES

	Charleston 1818-42 = 100	New Orleans 1824-42 = 100
1820	110	119
1830	82	86
1840	83	91
1850	87	103
1860	94	105

Source: See source note to table 23.

[a] The distinction between rural and urban refers to the area in which the owner of the slave resided when the slave was appraised or sold. Those slaves under the urban heading were almost always city slaves, with urban occupations.

[b] Numbers in parentheses are the number of slave appraisals or sales in the sample.

[c] Includes all slaves who were appraised.

[d] Excludes those slaves listed as being under 10 or over 55 years old, those who were sick, and those who were skilled.

[e] Richmond, Lynchburg, and Fredericksburg; 1820 figures are for Richmond alone.

[f] Refers to a twelve-month hire.

n.a.: not available.

for 1849 to 1851. The table also includes information about the data sources.

The most interesting feature of these price data is that they exhibit cycles similar to those found in the slave population figures. During those decades in which the aggregate slave population increased most slowly, prices increased fastest, and vice versa. Therefore, 1820 to 1830 and 1840 to 1850 were decades of declining or slowly rising slave prices, whereas the other two periods were decades of sharply increasing slave prices.

Slave prices did not equalize among regions during the period studied. They were substantially higher in the New South (Louisiana) than in the Old South states, although differences are diminished in the labor force figures. The labor force data obviously account for some heterogeneity in the data, because a larger percentage of slave appraisals in the New South were of slaves of working age. Nevertheless, there are differences even in slave labor prices between these regions. Some, if not all, of the differential is due to transportation costs. These costs include not only those of physically moving a slave, but also the working time lost in the interim. It has also been suggested that slaveowners were reluctant to sell a slave from a family unit to be moved to the New South.[13] In some cases this meant that in order to move a slave of prime age to the richer cotton regions of Louisiana, less productive members of the family would also have to be transported. This extra transport cost could certainly have widened the spread between prices in different areas. It should also be remembered that the New South was a rapidly expanding region. Given sufficient time, all prices would probably have come into equilibrium with the difference in prices just equaling that of transportation costs.

Table 23 also gives the rate of growth of rental or hire rates for rural states and a group of Virginia cities—Richmond, Lynchburg, and Fredericksburg. The data for these three cities, even after an attempt to adjust for skill differences, show a substantial rise in the rate of hire from 1850 to 1860. The data underlying this table, given in table 24, indicate that hire rates for these two areas were quite similar in 1850. The fact that urban slave rental rates were rising more rapidly than rural rates between 1850 and 1860 might appear strange because these cities were not gaining slaves rapidly during that period. One explanation for this observation is that there was a change in the skill mix in the cities.

Urban slaves may have become a more skilled group, as was suggested earlier.

Because price changes for one commodity can be the result of more general, nominal price changes, one must deflate by a price index. If the price of a particular good or service rose over time and the general price level increased as well, then the entire change in prices may have been due to monetary or aggregate demand factors. But had the price level for the economy or region been steady, then factors more specific to this one commodity would probably explain the observed change. Any price index will be imperfect, for the market basket used is usually incorrect for the researcher's particular purpose, and the region specified is usually too large or too small. I have used George Rogers Taylor's wholesale commodity price index for Charleston, and for New Orleans.[14] They do not differ substantially from each other, and both are somewhat similar to the well-known Warren and Pearson wholesale commodity price index. The Taylor New Orleans index rises more from 1830 to 1840 than that for Charleston, reflecting the boom experienced in the New South during that period. The New Orleans index is used to deflate the prices and hire rates for the New South, while that for Charleston is applied to Old South and Border State data.

The most important conclusion to be drawn from table 23 is that with few exceptions the deflated prices and hire rates for slaves had cycles similar to—though the inverse of—those for the urban and aggregate slave populations. To furnish an explanation for these cycles is one of the central objectives of chapter 5.

5 An Explanation
for the Relative Decline
of Urban Slavery:
The Formal Model

The evidence on the course of urban slave populations and prices presented in chapter 4 suggests the need for a
comprehensive model of the slave labor market which will aid in
explaining the relative decline in urban slavery. This model should
be consistent not only with population changes but also with
information on the demographic and skill characteristics of the
urban slave population. It should incorporate the relevant factors
which determine the demand for and supply of slave labor and
should consider the interaction of the urban and the rural sectors.

While it is easy to specify a complex model with many variables, the data required to estimate all of its parameters are not
available. However, by efficient design and careful manipulation
of the model, it is possible to make these meager data yield information on (1) differences in the rates of growth of the demand
for slaves between the urban and the rural sectors as well as
among particular cities, (2) differences in the elasticities of demand between the urban and the rural sectors as well as among
particular cities, and (3) some of the reasons for the difference
in both the growth rates and the elasticities. This information will,
in turn, make it possible to account for the puzzling feature
stressed in the previous chapter, such as the relative decline in the
urban slave population and its wide oscillations in rate-of-change
form.

The model which will be constructed is rather uncomplicated
but nonetheless technical. Much of its discussion might prove
difficult for those who do not understand price theory and econo-
metrics. But I believe that even the novice can grasp the essence
of this chapter, for I have tried to define most technical terms and
methods. Because the results of this exercise are essential to a
understanding of urban slavery and its relation to the antebellum
Southern economy, I have first presented a simplified version of

the model. Part 1 describes why the demand for urban slaves need not have been declining even during periods of decreasing urban slave quantities, and how one can view all four decades as part of a single process. Because it is a simplified presentation, it assumes rather than computes values for the elasticity of demand for slaves (that is, values for the responsiveness of quantity to changes in price, in percentage terms). The last few paragraphs of part 1 summarize the findings of part 2 for the less technical reader. Part 2 estimates demand functions for slaves to determine their exact form, without assuming values for the elasticity of demand. I urge all readers, regardless of economic and statistical skills, to read part 1 and at least to attempt part 2.

Part 1. A Simple Form of the Model

This model presents a simple way of conceptualizing the urban slave labor market over the period 1820–60. Only the demand function† for this labor will be considered to determine whether or not it was declining during this period or just parts of it. Because the demand relationship is static and the question addressed is dynamic, another form of the demand function will be considered—that which relates *changes* in quantities over time to *changes* in prices. It will be shown that with information about only prices and quantities of slaves, one can conclude that the demand for slaves was not steadily declining over the period. In fact, it was rising in most decades for the majority of cities. These conclusions are somewhat dependent on the values assigned to the various urban demand elasticities, that is, the responsiveness of quantity to changes in price. Part 2 of this chapter introduces a method of determining these values and then uses these estimates to analyze urban slavery and its relationship to the rural sector.

Because this model utilizes the concept of a demand function, one must first choose some specific functional form with which to work. I have chosen the constant elasticity†† version for simplicity.

---

†Recall that a demand function shows the maximum quantity, per unit time, consumers desire to purchase at any price, holding other relevant factors constant.

††The price elasticity of demand is the percentage change in the quantity which consumers purchase when prices change, say, 1 percent. It is expressed in percentages to be invariant to the units of measurement. Depending on the precise form of the demand function, this elasticity can change

Assume therefore that the demand function for slave labor in any particular city, i, during a decade is

(1) $$Q_i = D_i P_i^{-e_i} ,$$

where Q_i is the number of slaves demanded, D_i is an index of the level of demand and is a function of all factors on which Q_i depends, except P_i,† P_i is the price of a homogeneous slave labor input expressed either as a rental fee or a purchase price, and e_i is a positive number and is the (constant) price elasticity of demand.

For dealing with decade changes in Q, P, and D, it is convenient to express equation (1) in terms of rates of growth, that is, differentiate totally the logarithmic transformation of equation (1), to get:

(2) $$Q^*_i = D^*_i - e_i P^*_i ,$$

where an asterisk (*) accompanying any variable indicates the rate of growth of that variable over time. Solving equation (2) for D^*_i yields:

(3) $$D^*_i = Q^*_i + e_i P^*_i .$$

D^*_i measures the percentage shift in the demand schedule for slave labor in any city during a decade. If it is a positive number, then demand was growing; if it is negative, demand for slave labor in that particular city was declining. The value D^*_i can also be zero, in which case demand was stationary. Many historians who have argued that urban slavery was a dying institution explicitly or implicitly base their case on the assumption that D^*_i was less than zero.

The shift term D_i is a function of many variables. In this case the most important of these are: the level of value added or income per capita in the cities, to be denoted as V; the level of the free urban population, a proxy for the level of demand for domestic servants, Q_{fp}; the prices of substitutes and complements for urban slaves, of which the wage rate for free labor, P_f, is the mos

---

or remain constant as one moves along the demand schedule. The constant elasticity form assumes that the elasticity is the same, independent of one's position on the function, that is, regardless of how much consumers purchase.

†I will further specify D_i below. It is usually assumed to depend on income, population, and the prices of complements and substitutes.

important; and the dollar amount of license fees, badge costs, taxes, jailing costs, or any other costs specific to holding slaves in the cities, T.

The level of taxation, T, is the variable most frequently stressed in the traditional literature on the subject of urban slavery. The annual cost of using slaves must include their annual hire rate and the annual rate of taxes and other specifically urban costs of holding slaves. When P_i is measured, instead, by the purchase price of a slave, T is to be interpreted as the present value of taxes and other special costs. In either case, only if T grew over time could this variable have served to dampen the *growth* in demand for urban slaves. If the variables which make up T increased sufficiently, it is possible that the observed decline in urban slave quantities can be explained by increases in costs specific to using slaves in the city.

Adapting equation (1) to take into account the determinants of D_i yields:

$$(4) \qquad Q_i = D''_i V_i{}^{b_1} Q_{fp_i}{}^{b_2} P_{f_i}{}^{b_3} (P_i + T_i)^{-\epsilon_i}$$

where D''_i includes the effects of variables not explicitly defined in equation (4).† In this equation, T_i has been added to P_i to get the total per-unit time price of using slaves in the city. Both T_i and P_i should be expressed in the same dimension, either stock or flow, so that they can be summed.[1]

Differentiating equation (4) to express it in rate-of-growth form, and dropping the i subscripts, yields:

$$5) \qquad Q^* = [D''^* + b_1 V^* + b_2 Q^*_{fp} + b_3 P^*_f$$
$$- \frac{\epsilon \phi}{1 + \phi} T^*] - \frac{\epsilon}{1 + \phi} P^* ,$$

where $\phi = T/P$ that is, taxes as a percentage of price, and b_1 and b_2 are the elasticities of the two market-size variables. The value b_3 is the cross elasticity of demand for slave labor with respect to the price of free labor. This is normally expected to be a positive number to reflect the gross substitutability between the two laboring groups. The variables enclosed in brackets are the components of D^* and collectively determine the rate of change in demand.

---

†Note that the variables constituting D_i have also been expressed in constant elasticity form.

Note that the "true" elasticity is ϵ_i, which measures the responsiveness of quantity to changes in all aspects of price. The elasticity in equation (1), e_i, measures responsiveness only to changes in the direct payment, such as the net hire rate, and not to changes in the level of taxation.[2] The relation between the two elasticities is $e = [\epsilon/(1 + \phi)]$; therefore, if $T = 0$, then $\phi = 0$, and the coefficient on P^* becomes $-e$ as in equation (2). But if $T > 0$, any change in P will only affect part of the price for slave labor services, and therefore the coefficient ϵ will be reduced by the ratio $[1/1 + \phi]$. Secondary historical literature on this subject points to the possibility that not only was $T > 0$ but also that $T^* > 0$; taxes were positive and were growing over time. If correct, the T term served to dampen the growth in the quantity of slave services demanded. But its overall effect still depends on the magnitude of ϕ. The smaller was ϕ, the smaller the effect on Q^* of a particular value of T^*. Therefore, the smaller the percentage of total price accounted for by taxes, the smaller the changes in slave quantities affected by changes in taxes.[3]

Much can be gleaned about the magnitude and sign (positive or negative) of the D^*_i's even from the simple model expressed by equation (3). Equation (3) states that with information on P^*_i, Q^*_i, and e_i, the value D^*_i can be calculated. This is remarkable, for in order to determine whether demand was declining or rising, all we need is information on the trend of slave quantities and prices over time and the price elasticity of demand. Even though we lack information on the magnitude of the latter variable e_i, knowledge of its sign[4] (positive) and the data presented in chapter 4 on Q^*_i and P^*_i enable one to state minimum or maximum values for the D^*_i. This important point can be demonstrated quite easily with reference to figure 2, the axes of which are P^* and Q^*, the rate of change in slave prices and quantities.[5]

Suppose an observation for a particular city during a specific decade has both a positive Q^*_i and positive P^*_i, so that the point corresponding to that observation falls in quadrant 1. Then D^* must also have been positive for that city during that decade, for no negatively sloped function of the form expressed in equation (2) can be drawn both to include a point such as A and to intersect the Q^* axis in its negative range. Point A in fig. 2 refers to Richmond during 1850–60, where the P^*_i is the rate of change in deflated slave prices for the three Virginia cities (Fredericksburg

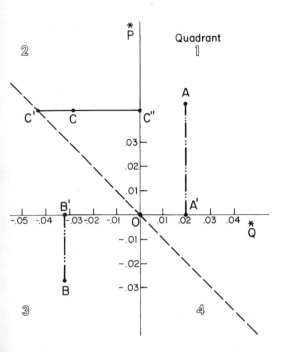

Figure 2. A Simple Graphical Explanation of the Computation of $D*_i$

Petersburg, and Richmond) for 1850 to 1860, and the $Q*_i$ is the rate of change in the Richmond slave labor force for that decade. Not only is it obvious from equation (3) that $D*_i$ must have been positive for Richmond during 1850–60, but it also follows that $D*_i$ must have been larger than the amount measured by the distance $0A'$, that is, the rate of growth of $Q*_i$ per year, or 2.0 percent per year. *In other words, growth in demand must have been positive if slaves were drawn into a city despite a rising price.* Therefore, all observations such as A which fall in quadrant 1 refer unambiguously to cases of growing demand, and minimum values of the $D*_i$'s can be ascertained with only information concerning the sign of the elasticity of demand.

Consider, instead, an observation such as B, which refers to New Orleans for 1840 to 1850. In this case both $P*_i$ and $Q*_i$ are negative, and the point falls in quadrant 3. All such observations unambiguously refer to cases of declining demand, and, using the example of point B, demand must have been declining by an amount greater than $0B'$, that is, the rate of decline of the slave population, or 3.2 percent per year. This is, *if a city lost slaves despite a falling price, demand must have been falling.*

In contrast to these two sets of unambiguous results, all points which fall in quadrants 2 and 4 have D^*_i's of unknown sign and magnitude. In these cases the D^*_i's can be deduced only if the size of the elasticity of demand is known. However, even rough notions about the elasticity of demand, e, can clear up some of the ambiguity for these cases. Consider point C, in quadrant 2, which refers to a case of decreasing quantity and increasing price, such as that of Washington between 1830 and 1840. In the absence of information on e, nothing could be said about the nature of D^*_i in this case except that it could not have been declining by more than the distance CC'', the rate of decline in quantity. However, if we knew the elasticity of demand, we could be much more precise. For example, if e was approximately unity, then demand must have been growing by approximately $C'C$. The diagonal line $C'E^*$ has a slope of unity, and the inverse of the slope of this line measures the price elasticity. This is because the price elasticity of demand $e =$ (percentage change in Q)/(percentage change in P) $= Q^*/P^*$, and the slope of the line is P^*/Q^*. In fact, if e were unity for all cities and for every decade, then all points above the diagonal would refer to observations of increasing demand, and all points below the diagonal would correspond to observations of decreasing demand.

A Prima Facie Case

The procedure suggested above has been applied to the forty data points on slave prices and quantities given in table 25 and graphed in fig. 3. Each observation refers to a particular city's average annual rate of change in its slave labor force for a specific decade matched with the average annual rate of change in deflated slave prices for the area closest to that city. Recall from chapter 4 that price data could not be assembled for all cities and all states and that one has therefore to decide which price series to use for each of the ten cities in the sample. Selecting the correct price for Richmond's slaves was a simple task, since slave price data were collected for the three Virginia cities—Fredericksburg, Lynchburg,

TABLE 25   Average Annual Rates of Change in Slave Labor Forces and Prices for Ten Cities over Four Decades

City (City Code)	1820-30		1830-40		1840-50		1850-60	
	Q^{*a}	P^{*b}	Q^{*}	P^{*}	Q^{*}	P^{*}	Q^{*}	P^{*}
Baltimore[c] (b)	.004	.019	-.023	.043	-.006	-.004	-.032	.046
Charleston[d] (c)	.018	-.016	.000	.034	.031	-.009	-.033	.054
Louisville[c] (l)	.098	.019	.031	.043	.049	-.004	-.012	.046
Mobile[e] (m)	.037	.003	.122	.029	.054	-.028	.010	.063
New Orleans[e] (no)	.015	.003	.097	.029	-.032	-.028	-.019	.063
Norfolk[c] (n)	.014	.019	.000	.043	.022	-.004	-.027	.046
Richmond[c] (r)	.044	.019	.025	.043	.026	-.004	.020	.046
Saint Louis[e] (t)	.045	.003	-.052	.029	.060	-.028	-.062	.063
Savannah[f] (s)	.032	-.019	.013	.060	.032	-.005	.016	.032
Washington[c] (w)	.026	.019	-.028	.043	.021	-.004	-.016	.046

Sources: Tables 16 and 23.

[a]Average annual rates of change in city slave labor force, from table 16.
[b]Average annual rates of change in slave prices, in deflated form, from table 23.
[c]Virginia city (Fredericksburg, Lynchburg, and Richmond) slave prices, deflated.
[d]Charleston slave prices, deflated.
[e]Louisiana slave labor force prices, deflated.
[f]Georgia slave prices, deflated.

and Richmond. The same prices were similarly used for Baltimore, Norfolk, Louisville, and Washington, since these cities were close to the Virginia market. Charleston data were used only for Charleston. Georgia rural prices were used for Savannah, and rural Louisiana slave labor force prices for New Orleans and Mobile. These Louisiana prices were also used for Saint Louis because the economic activity of this city was probably greatly affected by the Mississippi River and delta traffic. In all cases, the prices given in table 25 and represented in fig. 3 are deflated by the appropriate regional price indices.

The ten cities and four decades yield forty observations, which are graphically shown in fig. 3. The code used on the graph corresponds to the letters in parentheses in table 25; for instance, no_1 refers to the New Orleans observation for 1820 to 1830, and b_3 to Baltimore, 1840 to 1850. Table 26 lists the quadrants in which

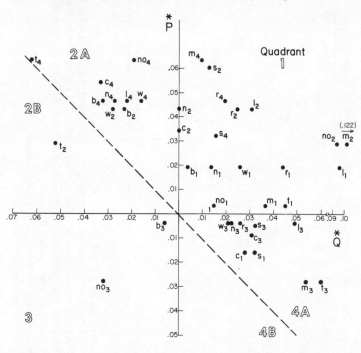

Figure 3. Forty Observations on the Rate of Growth of Slave Labor Forces and Prices for each of Ten Cities over Four Decades (see table 25)

the observations are located and divides the points in quadrants 2 and 4 into those which lie above the diagonal and those which lie below it. That is, it separates points using the criterion of a unitary elasticity of demand.

TABLE 26   Simple Determination of D^*_i, Corresponding to Figure 2

City	1820-30	1830-40	1840-50	1850-60
Baltimore	+[a]	2 A[b]	-[c]	2 A
Charleston	4 A[d]	+	4 A	2 A
Louisville	+	+	4 A	2 A
Mobile	+	+	4 A	+
New Orleans	+	+	-	2 A
Norfolk	+	+	4 A	2 A
Richmond	+	+	4 A	+
Saint Louis	+	2 B[e]	4 A	2 A
Savannah	4 A	+	4 A	+
Washington	+	2 A	4 A	2 A

Source: Table 25.
  [a]Quadrant 1.
  [b]Quadrant 2 above diagonal.
  [c]Quadrant 3.
  [d]Quadrant 4 above diagonal.
  [e]Quadrant 2 below diagonal.

From the previous analysis it was shown that the location of the points in the quadrants determines whether or not demand was unambiguously rising or falling. Only if an observation was in quadrant 3 could one be certain that slave demand was falling during that particular decade and in that specific city. For the data in this study, only two observations fall in quadrant 3. In only these two cases did demand unambiguously decline, and one of these points, that for Baltimore 1840–50, lies barely below the origin in quadrant 3. Employing the tentative assumption that the elasticity of demand was unity across all cities and all decades yields only one observation out of the remaining thirty-eight, which represents a case of declining demand. This observation, which is for Saint Louis 1830–40, is the only one that falls below the diagonal but not in quadrant 3. Nineteen observations lie in quadrants 2A and 4A, that is, above the diagonal, though not in quadrant 1. Eighteen points fall in quadrant 1 and are therefore cases of strictly increasing slave demand functions.

Thus it appears from this simple determination of the $D*_i$'s that typically the demand for urban slaves was increasing in the South. In fact, during the 1850s, when according to many historians demand was weakest, no observations indicate declining demand if the elasticity of demand were unity. This elementary determination of the sign of the $D*_i$'s creates a prima facie case against a theory of declining demand and, therefore, against the simple notion that urban slaves were "pushed" out of the cities, especially during the 1850s.

This conclusion, which will be substantiated further in part 2 by the use of more elaborate techniques, is important not just for understanding urban slavery but also for analyzing antebellum Southern economic development. It appears from these results that city slaves were not necessarily removed from the cities by internal pressures, for the demand for their labor was steadily rising. Instead, urban slaveowners sold their laborers during certain periods of rapidly rising prices, as in the much discussed decade 1850–60. This period, during which slave quantities declined in most cities, does not now appear to suggest that slavery stifled the development of the South by reducing the level of urbanization. It will be shown that the clue to understanding how declines in urban slave quantities can be consistent with rapid growth of demand is the difference in the magnitude of the urban and rural price elasticities of demand. The greater ability of urban labor demanders to substitute free for slave workers appears to explain many of the apparent anomalies in the data.

Part 2 of chapter 5 will be directed toward estimating these elasticities, the values of which have been merely assumed in part 1. After these elasticities have been computed, they will be used to explain more fully the characteristics of the data which were stressed in chapter 4.

The elasticity of demand will be estimated by fitting demand functions to the data which have been presented in table 25 and graphed in fig. 3. The econometric technique used is called ordinary least squares regression analysis, and it consists of fitting a line to points by minimizing the sum of the squared deviations or residuals from the line. In fig. 4 the line (labeled C) has been fit by "eyeballing" the four hypothetical data points, that is the x's. (Since I am fitting functions to only four points, I could use the simpler technique of graphing. But that would be somewhat inaccurate, and, in addition, the more sophisticated method shows what would have to be done if more observations were available.) The inverse of the slope of this line is the elasticity of demand. In part 2, I estimate such an elasticity for every city, for three urban aggregates, and for the total United States.

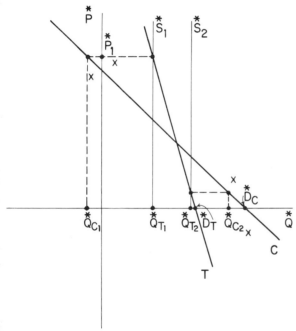

Figure 4. A Graphical Representation of the Expanded Form of the Model. The demand and supply functions drawn in this diagram are in growth rate form, and the axes are P^* and Q^*, not P and Q. Although these functions differ from more conventional demand and supply schedules, they are related to them, as equations (1) and (2) show. The demand function given in growth rate form in (2) is actually a more conventional demand function, as in (1), growing at a constant rate. The rate at which it is growing is given by its intersection with the horizontal or Q^* axis. The price elasticity of demand is given by the inverse of the slope of the rate-of-growth demand function.

Note that in estimating the urban demand elasticities I have assumed that price changes are given to the cities and that all price and quantity pairs therefore determine a demand function. If this were not the case, the model would have to be more elaborate to account for the determination of price *and* quantity changes simultaneously. The demand function for all slaves in the United States was estimated under the reverse assumption. I have assumed that the supply of slaves over short periods of time was highly unresponsive to changes in price, that is, it had a zero elasticity of supply. Therefore, rather than being faced with price changes, the aggregate demanders are given quantity changes and determine price. The total demand for slaves in rate-of-change form has been drawn in fig. 4 and labeled T, and two zero elastic supply functions (S^*_1 and S^*_2) are also included in the graph.

I have deliberately drawn the T function with a steeper slope than the C function. This reflects the results of the regression analysis, which yield higher elasticity values for the cities than for the total. The two supply functions are different because the rate-of-change in the total slave population differed among the various decades, as discussed in chapter 4.

The impact of these different elasticities and the varying supply function on changes in the urban slave population can be seen quite easily. The equilibrium rate of change in slave prices is determined for any decade by the intersection of, say, S^*_1 with T. This reflects the assumption made previously that supply is given to the South as a whole, and that price (or the rate of change of price) is determined by the total demand. This rate of change of price (P^*_1) is then given to the cities, which determines how they will change their slave quantity ($Q^*_{c_1}$). Because the elasticity of demand for urban slaves was greater than that for rural slaves, the cities responded more violently to price changes. That is, $Q^*_{c_1}$ and $Q^*_{c_2}$ bracket $Q^*_{T_1}$ and $Q^*_{T_2}$. Thus, a highly plausible reason for the extreme variations in urban slave labor forces is their greater elasticity of demand.

Notice that $Q^*_{c_1}$ is negative; that is, the quantity of urban slaves declined during that period of time. But the city slave demand function in rate of change form (C) intersects the Q^* axis at a positive point (D^*_c). This intersection point measures the shift term or the amount by which the urban demand for slaves was growing. As can be seen in the graph, $D*_C > D*_T$, even though $Q*_{C_1}$ is negative. Therefore, it is *possible* that urban demand was increasing quite rapidly even during periods of declining quantities, such as the 1850s. Computation of these demand functions in part 2 enables an empirical test of this point.

In the remainder of part 2, some of the assumptions of the simple model are dropped, and differences among the cities are analyzed. First, the assumption about a constant rate of change shift term, $D*_i$, is eliminated. The result is a complex interaction of both changing urban demands over the decades and the larger urban elasticity, which provide complementary explanations for the quantity data. Second, the course of slave prices is viewed within this context of changing demands. Next, the differences among the various cities are stressed, and plausible explanations for these dissimilarities are given.

Part 2. An Expanded Form of the Model: Estimates of the Elasticity of Demand

Although a prima facie case has been presented in part 1 against the declining demand hypothesis, too many observations in fig. 3 fall in quadrants 2A and 4A to warrant an arbitrary assumption about the demand elasticity. In addition, precise estimates of this parameter are necessary for a more thorough explanation of the course of urban slavery. Rather than speculating about the value of the shift terms, their *exact* magnitude could be calculated by using equation (3), if the demand elasticities were known. Furthermore, this simple but suggestive analysis does not aid in explaining the important phenomena stressed in chapter 4, such as the population cycles and other demographic changes.

Although there are only four observations for each city, these data are still useful in providing at least a rough notion of the magnitude of the elasticity of demand for slave labor in the cities. I have made two principal estimates of these elasticities by fitting demand equations using ordinary least squares. The first estimate uses equation (2) as the underlying model,

$$(2) \qquad Q*_i = D*_i - e_i P*_i \quad .$$

In making estimates for each city using equation (2), the shift terms, the $D*_i$'s, are assumed to have been constant from decade to decade, as are the e_i's, the elasticities of demand. In addition,

since the cities were such a small fraction of the slave labor
market, they are assumed to have faced an infinitely elastic supply
function for slave labor. That is, each city's supply of slave labor
is a horizontal line at the given price, implying that any quantity
of labor can be purchased at the going price. This eliminates si-
multaneity problems by making the price variable exogenous, in
this case determined by the larger rural market.

In the second set of estimates I have attempted to include a
variable to account for major market size effects. Since the data
consist of only four observations for each city, only one variable,
other than price and the constant term, could be included. The
variable selected is $Q^*_{fp_i}$, the annual percentage rate of change of
a city's free population, and the new equation is of the following
form:

$$(6) \qquad Q^*_i = D'^*_i + b\, Q^*_{fp_i} - e_i P^*_i \ .$$

The variable $Q^*_{fp_i}$ can be interpreted as a proxy for the rate of
growth of economic activity in the cities. It also serves as an estimate of the rate of growth in the demand for slave domestic services. But it is, unfortunately, only a partial measure and misses,
for example, economic changes not accompanied by population
movements. A better measure would be per-capita income or value
added in the city, but data limitations prevented their use.

These demand equations should also include a term for the rate
of change in the wage rate paid to free laborers. Such data are
also not available, and the limited number of observations would
have precluded their addition in any case. To the extent that these
laborers were gross substitutes for slaves, the estimated slave price
elasticity of demand has a downward bias.[6] Another omitted variable is what was previously denoted as T^*, that is, the rate of
change of taxes, license fees, badge costs, jailing fines, and so on.
This variable does not appear to have been important and is
omitted from the regressions because of the limited number of
observations. The magnitude of T also affects the estimated elasticity of demand for slave labor services. That is, if ϕ, or T/P
(see equation [5]) were positive and large, the estimate of the
elasticity of demand would be downward biased. This stems from
the fact that the estimation procedure yields $[\epsilon/(1 + \phi)] = e$,
although the true parameter value is ϵ. Moreover, the rate of

change in the variable T, denoted as T^*, affects the interpretation of D^*. Both points will be discussed further in this chapter.

The aggregate slave demand function was empirically estimated in a somewhat different fashion from that for the cities. It was assumed that, in the aggregate, the supply of slave labor was determined exogenously, or, equivalently, that the elasticity of supply for slave labor was zero.[7] This results in slave prices being determined solely by the aggregate demand function. These slave prices are then used in the urban equation for the allocation of slave labor between the urban and the rural sectors.

The aggregate demand for slaves is given by

$$(7) \qquad Q_t = D_t P_t^{-e_t} \quad .$$

Differentiating the logarithmic transformation of (7) yields:

$$(8) \qquad Q^*_t = D^*_t - e_t P^*_t \quad .$$

In computing the regressions, the price-dependent form of this equation was used, in line with the assumption of an exogenously determined Q^*_t. This is given by:

$$(9) \qquad P^*_t = (D^*_t/e_t) - (Q^*_t/e_t).$$

Equation (9) was estimated again by ordinary least squares using a weighted average of the deflated rural Virginia and rural Louisiana prices for P^*_t. A combination of the two price series was employed because the Old South at the beginning of the period was the largest slave-trading market but declined in importance as the New South—Alabama, Arkansas, Louisiana, Mississippi, Missouri, and Texas—expanded. The weights placed on the Virginia and Louisiana prices represent the relative importance of the two areas as measured by the number of slaves residing in each.[8] These weighted prices seem a more reasonable measure of aggregate slave value than any single regional price series.

The shift parameter in the aggregate equation can be construed as a function of all variables affecting quantity other than price. In one form of this simple model it is assumed to be constant across decades, but in a more complete model it should be expressed as a function of market size and substitution factors. The most important of the market-size factors was probably the deflated value of cotton produced in the South, C, and a second form of this equation given by

(10) $P^*_t = (\frac{1}{e})_t D'^*_t + (\frac{b}{e})_t C^* - (\frac{1}{e})_t Q^*_t$,

was also estimated. The new constant term, D'^*_t, is a function of all variables other than the rate of change in both quantity and the value of cotton production. The symbols b, e, D^*, and D'^* will be used to represent both urban and rural parameters; the i and t subscripts will be removed for convenience.

The demand parameters for rural slaves can be computed from the estimates for the aggregate and urban equations. It can be shown that if the city demand function for slaves, expressed in rate-of-growth form, can be written as

(11) $Q^*_c = D^*_c - e_cP^*$,

and the rural demand function as

(12) $Q^*_r = D^*_r - e_rP^*$,

then the demand function for all slaves can be written as

(13) $Q^*_t = [\alpha D^*_r + (1 - \alpha)D^*_c]$
              $- [\alpha e_r + (1 - \alpha)e_c]P^*$.

That is, the shift term for the aggregate demand function is a convex combination or a weighted average of the shift terms for the rural and city functions. The weight, α, is the share of the total slaves who resided in rural areas, that is, $[Q_r/Q_t]$. The aggregate elasticity is also a convex combination of the price elasticities for rural and urban slaves, again weighted by α. Therefore, since

(14) $D^*_t = \alpha D^*_r + (1 - \alpha)D^*_c$,

estimation of D^*_t and D^*_c, with knowledge of α, can yield D^*_r.

Equations (2), (6), (9), and (10) were estimated using ordinary least squares. The error terms in all equations are assumed to enter linearly and have the required properties but have been surpressed for ease of exposition in writing all equations. Both the city and aggregate regressions were run using the rate of change in the slave population and labor force alternatively as the estimate of Q^*_i and Q^*_t. Since the labor force data were extracted by a sampling procedure from the manuscript census schedules (see chapter 4), they are subject to more error than are the population figures. But since the labor force figures are more appropriate for a model of the labor market, the results stemming from those data have been used throughout the remainder of this chapter.

The results of the regression runs given in table 27 are impressive.[9] All coefficients are in the range of reasonable estimates for the shift terms, and the elasticities are negative with the exceptions of a positive elasticity for New Orleans and the New South cities in the nonextended form of the model. Furthermore, the results are consistent across cities, with values for $\hat{e}_i$ ranging from 0.124 to 1.778, using the results in part C of the table. As was noted before, the estimates of the price elasticities of demand are biased downward because of the exclusion of the substitute labor price term and the multiplication by the $[1/1 + \phi]$ factor.

Due to the limitations on the number of observations, these results ought to be highly sensitive to the data series used. In an earlier work[10] I used a slightly different data series for the price variable and deflated by the Warren and Pearson wholesale price index, instead of Taylor's New Orleans and Charleston series. These results, surprisingly enough, do not differ substantially from those in table 27 in terms of coefficient magnitude but were in general more significant, that is, their "t" values were larger.

It can be seen from table 27 that the elasticity of demand for urban slaves varied with city. In general, the Border State cities had the highest elasticity values, and those in the New South the lowest. During the period studied, the Border State cities had the largest pool of substitute labor for slaves among all the cities studied, which could account for the higher elasticity. In addition, slaves in these cities appear to have been less skilled than those in the Old and New South areas and therefore more easily substituted in response to changes in price. Even though elasticities differ by city, it is important to note that *the elasticity estimates, in part C of table 27, for each city are substantially higher than that for all slave states. This is a crucial difference and is central in explaining the large slave population cycles which the cities experienced.*

The rate of growth in demand for urban slaves appears to have been large. Estimation of the simple model, equation (2), indicates that the rate of growth in urban slave demand for two of the urban aggregates was greater than the rate for all slave states and that the rate for the third group of cities was quite close in magnitude to that for all slave states.[11] The only city which shows a

negative rate of growth in demand for any form of the equation is
Baltimore, and this negative rate becomes zero when the labor
force is used instead of population as the dependent variable.

The expanded form of the model, that is the regression results
of equation (6) presented in table 27, parts C and D, is quite
interesting in determining the effects of one of the components of
D^*. The variable Q^*_{fp} was included to account for some of the
change in demand due to market size factors. But this variable
can have an additional effect, for white labor was both a demander
of slave labor and a substitute for it. Although in the first instance
the expected sign of $\hat{b}$ is positive, it could be negative under the
conditions outlined below. In general, the reason for including
Q^*_{fp} was to pick up market-size effects, but the results indicate
that the rate of growth in the free population has also incorporated substitution factors.

This interpretation of $\hat{b}$ can be seen by considering the expanded
form of the model, or equation

$$(5) \qquad Q^* = [D''^* + b_1 V^* + b_2 Q^*_{fp} + b_3 P^*_f$$
$$- \frac{\epsilon\phi}{1 + \phi}\, T^*] - \frac{\epsilon}{1 + \phi}\, P^* .$$

All b_i coefficients are expected to have positive signs. If V^* (the
rate of change in value added or income per capita) and P^*_f
(the rate of change in the wage of free labor) are not included in
the estimated model because of data limitations, specification bias
enters in the following way. Consider V^* as a function of Q^*_{fp};
then $V^* = \lambda Q^*_{fp} + u$, where $\lambda > 0$ and u contains all other factors on which V^* depends uncorrelated with Q^*_{fp}. In addition,
consider the determination of P^*_f in the substitute or free labor
market. In some very simple model of such a market one of the
reduced form equations might look like: $P^*_f = \eta Q^*_{fp} + w$, where
$\eta < 0$ and is the own price elasticity of demand for the substitute
labor, and w contains all other factors important in this model
which are uncorrelated with Q^*_{fp}. Substituting into equation (5)
the two equations for V^* and P^*_f yields:

$$(5') \qquad Q^* = [D''^* + b_1 u + b_3 w + (\lambda b_1 + b_2$$
$$+ \eta b_3)Q^*_{fp} - \frac{\epsilon\phi}{1 + \phi}\, T^*] - \frac{\epsilon}{1 + \phi}\, P^* .$$

TABLE 27   An Empirical Estimation of the Model for Ten Cities, Three Urban Aggregates, and All Slave States

A. $\overset{*}{Q}$ = average annual rate of change in slave labor force.

Regressions run in the form: $\overset{*}{Q} = \overset{*}{D} - e\overset{*}{P}$,

for cities and urban aggregates;

$\overset{*}{P} = \frac{1}{e}\overset{*}{D} - \frac{1}{e}\overset{*}{Q}$, for all slave states.

	$\hat{\overset{*}{D}}$	$-\hat{e}$	R^2
All slave states[a]	.027 (2.96)[b]	-.095 (-2.74)	.789
Baltimore[c]	.000 (.02)	-.549 (-1.73)	.599
Charleston[d]	.016 (2.17)	-.760 (-3.41)	.853
Louisville[c]	.071 (1.93)	-1.138 (-1.01)	.340
Mobile[e]	.059 (1.84)	-.224 (-.26)	.033
New Orleans[e]	.010 (.25)	.338 (.33)	.051
Norfolk[c]	.018 (1.52)	-.673 (-1.90)	.642
Richmond[c]	.034 (3.44)	-.172 (-.58)	.145
Saint Louis[e]	.023 (1.36)	-1.520 (-3.38)	.851
Savannah[f]	.028 (13.74)	-.274 (-4.77)	.919
Washington[c]	.027 (1.96)	-.993 (-2.42)	.745
Old South cities[c]	.031 (4.25)	-.654 (-2.97)	.816
New South cities[e]	.019 (.53)	.254 (.27)	.034
Border State cities[c]	.036 (2.83)	-1.178 (-3.03)	.821

TABLE 27—*Continued*

B. $\overset{*}{Q}$ = average annual rate of change in slave population[g]

Regressions run as in part A.

	$\overset{*}{\hat{D}}$	$-\hat{e}$	R^2
All slave states	.025 (6.72)	-.077 (-6.29)	.952
Baltimore	-.005 (-.96)	-.439 (-2.55)	.765
Charleston	.015 (2.55)	-.793 (-4.52)	.911
Louisville	.064 (2.00)	-.969 (-.99)	.330
Mobile[h]	.060 (2.05)	-.338 (-.46)	.097
New Orleans[h]	.013 (.35)	.111 (.12)	.007
Norfolk	.025 (.38)	-.814 (-.91)	.733
Richmond	.032 (4.59)	-.298 (-1.39)	.493
Saint Louis[h]	.015 (.24)	-1.259 (-1.45)	.754
Savannah	.025 (20.92)	-.146 (-4.24)	.900
Washington	.024 (2.17)	-1.007 (-2.99)	.818
Old South cities	.029 (4.26)	-.664 (-3.26)	.842
New South cities[h]	.023 (.66)	.057 (.07)	.002
Border State cities	.032 (3.47)	-1.093 (-3.92)	.885

TABLE 27—*Continued*

C. $\overset{*}{Q}$ = average annual rate of change in slave labor force.[i]

Regressions run in the form: $\overset{*}{Q} = \overset{*}{D}' + b\,\overset{*}{Q}_{fp} - e\overset{*}{P}$, for

the cities and urban aggregates, where $\overset{*}{Q}_{fp}$ = average

annual rate of change in the free population; and

$\overset{*}{P} = \dfrac{1}{e}\overset{*}{D}' + \dfrac{b}{e}\overset{*}{C} - \dfrac{1}{e}\overset{*}{Q}$, for all slave states, where

$\overset{*}{C}$ = average annual rate of change in the value of

cotton production.[j]

	$\hat{\overset{*}{D}}'$	$\hat{b}$	$-\hat{e}$	R^2
All slave states	.023 (2.40)	.061 (.56)	−.084 (−2.22)	.839
Baltimore	.074 (2.29)	−1.627 (−2.32)	−1.376 (−3.45)	.937
Charleston	.013 (.67)	.101 (.15)	−.719 (−1.74)	.856
Louisville	−.100 (−2.12)	2.018 (3.77)	−.462 (−1.04)	.957
Mobile	.016 (.91)	.789 (3.59)	−.535 (−1.59)	.930
New Orleans	−.026 (−.67)	.862 (1.46)	−.163 (−.18)	.700
Norfolk	.025 (.38)	−.061 (−.03)	−.814 (−.91)	.733
Richmond	.065 (2.47)	−1.063 (−1.26)	−.124 (−1.26)	.671
Saint Louis	.023 (.50)	−.011 (−.02)	−1.53 (−2.02)	.851
Savannah	.028 (5.01)	.000 (.00)	−.274 (−2.35)	.919
Washington	.032 (.39)	−.102 (−.07)	−1.030 (−1.28)	.746
Old South cities	.059 (8.99)	−.885 (−4.59)	−.919 (−10.46)	.992
New South cities	−.017 (−.52)	.832 (1.74)	−.212 (−.29)	.760
Border State cities	.096 (7.87)	−.979 (−5.11)	−1.778 (−11.24)	.993

TABLE 27—*Continued*

D. $\overset{\star}{Q}$ = average annual rate of change in slave population.[g]

Regressions run as in part C.

	$\hat{\overset{\star}{D}}{}'$	b	-e	R^2
All slave states	.027 (10.69)	-.044 (-2.02)	-.077 (-9.95)	.991
Baltimore	.037 (3.78)	-.936 (-4.40)	-.915 (-7.57)	.989
Charleston	.013 (.80)	.080 (.15)	-.761 (-2.34)	.913
Louisville	-.089 (-4.09)	1.800 (7.34)	-.366 (-1.80)	.988
Mobile[h]	.018 (1.26)	.731 (4.20)	-.475 (-1.96)	.951
New Orleans[h]	-.022 (-.48)	.768 (1.19)	-.170 (-.19)	.588
Norfolk	.032 (.48)	-.491 (-.22)	-.840 (-.92)	.658
Richmond	.051 (2.19)	-.633 (-.85)	-.269 (-1.16)	.705
Saint Louis[h]	.006 (.08)	.110 (.16)	-1.09 (-1.12)	.669
Savannah	.023 (17.47)	.115 (2.35)	-.192 (-7.03)	.985
Washington	.017 (.26)	.139 (.11)	-.957 (-1.46)	.820
Old South cities	.056 (46.22)	-.837 (-23.85)	-.914 (-57.16)	.999
New South cities[h]	-.012 (-.32)	.736 (1.42)	-.199 (-.28)	.670
Border State cities	.074 (5.40)	-.681 (-3.19)	-1.511 (-8.58)	.990

TABLE 27—*Continued*

Source: See text.

[a]A weighted average of rural Virginia and Louisiana deflated prices was used, where the weights attached to the prices are the share in the total slave labor force of the Upper and Lower South regions. These price data in average annual rate-of-growth form are: 1820–30, $-.0104$; 1830–40, $.0468$; 1840–50, $-.0090$; 1850–60, $.0638$.

[b]Figures in parentheses, for all parts of this table, are "t" values. The "t" statistics for the aggregate equation coefficients are for $(\widehat{D/e})^*$ and $(\widehat{1/e})$. Confidence intervals for $\hat{D}^*$ and $\hat{e}$ can be computed for a given level of significance using this information.

[c]Deflated prices for Virginia cities used.

[d]Deflated prices for Charleston used.

[e]Deflated prices for Louisiana labor force used.

[f]Deflated prices for Georgia used.

[g]Prices used are the same for part A except where noted.

[h]Deflated prices for Louisiana used.

[i]Prices used are the same for part A.

[j]Cotton production is valued at New Orleans prices deflated by Taylor's wholesale price index for New Orleans. The reported data are for cotton values contemporaneous with the other data. Runs using lagged cotton values resulted in coefficients trivially different from these. For cotton production figures and prices see *Cotton and the Growth of the American Economy: Sources and Readings*, ed. Stuart Bruchey. The "t" statistics are given for $(\widehat{D/e})^*$, $(\widehat{b/e})$, and $(\widehat{1/e})$, respectively. Confidence intervals around $\hat{D}'^*$, $\hat{e}$, and $\hat{b}$ can be constructed for a given level of significance.

It is now obvious that b, the coefficient on Q^*_{fp} from equation (6), can be negative or positive depending on the relative strength of η and λ. The term η would be large, for example, if other factors were easily substitutable for free labor. The λ term would be large, for example, if additions to the free population were of high-income persons who would raise per-capita income. In addition, $\hat{D}'^*$ will be biased, because it includes terms $(b_1u + b_3w)$ from the V^* and P^*_f equations.

The results in part C of table 27 show that Baltimore, Norfolk, Richmond, Washington, and two of the urban aggregates have negative coefficients on Q^*_{fp}. This indicates that for these cities $|\eta b_3| > |\lambda b_1 + b_2|$. The own elasticity of demand for substitute labor was large, and the cross elasticity of demand between the two laboring groups was also high.

The inclusion of the Q^*_{fp} term for some cities reduces the constant, $\hat{D}'^*$. This term is construed as the agglomeration of all other shift factors. These cities have positive coefficients on Q^*_{fp}, that is, $|\eta b_3| < |\lambda b_1 + b_2|$. The results for Louisville and New Orleans show that market-size factors were so strong that some other components of D^* must have inhibited the growth of urban slavery, for $\hat{D}'^* < 0$. Possible factors accounting for the sign of the constant term are license fees, taxes, and other costs specific to holding slaves in the cities, although the discussion in chapter 3 has discounted this possibility.

A further bias can enter this work because of specification error due to the exclusion of the V^* variable. The $\hat{D}'^*$ term in equation (6) may be biased downward because of this omission, although the result crucially depends on the relation between migration and V^*. The quantity Q^*_{fp} includes the number of migrants, which was probably a positive function of V^* (as has been found for interstate migration).[12] But the other component of Q^*_{fp}, the natural rate of increase in the free population, can be assumed to have been independent of V^*. (It is only necessary that a part of the natural rate of increase be independent of V^*.) As a result, the estimate of b will be biased upward and that of D'^*_i downward, since part of Q^*_{fp} will reflect, not an increase in per-capita value added or income, but exogenous population growth.

The addition of a term for the rate of change in the deflated value of cotton production in the aggregate regressions (see table 27, part C) lowers the residual shift term. The demand for slaves in all slave states would have increased at a rate of about 2.3 percent per year even if the change in the value of cotton production had been zero. This peculiar result is insensitive to using a lagged value of cotton production. It may represent the fact that slaves were employed in uses other than cotton production on plantations but is more likely the result of employing too simple an econometric model for a complex set of interactions.

The Relationship Between the Urban Sector and the Countryside: A Two-Sector Analysis

Part of the analysis of the elasticity differences stressed above can be expedited by reducing the information contained in table 27 to two sectors—rural and urban. By viewing the interaction between the two sectors, one can use the regression results to determine the factors bearing on slave prices and quantities. In the remaining part of this chapter, the disaggregated urban results are used to analyze differences among the cities.

By combining the three urban aggregate demand curves in part C of table 27, one can obtain

$$(11')\qquad Q^*_c = D^*_c - e_c P^*_c \quad,$$

the total urban demand function.[13]

The shift term and the elasticity in equation $(11')$ are weighted averages of those for the three regions, where the weights are the average share of each region in the total urban slave population during the forty-year period.[14] The shift term for each region was constructed by multiplying the coefficient on Q^*_{fp}, or $\hat{b}$, by the mean of Q^*_{fp} and then adding to it the value of $\hat{D}'^*$. Substituting in equation $(11')$ these constructed parameter values yields:

$$(15)^{15}\qquad Q^*_c = .036 - .86\,P^*_c \quad.$$

The total equation (8) and the urban demand curve (15) together imply a rural demand curve,

$$(12')^{16}\qquad Q^*_r = D^*_r - e_r P^*_r \quad.$$

The parameter values for the total equation given in table 27, part C, yield a demand function for the aggregate of the form

$$(16)^{17}\qquad Q^*_t = .026 - .08\,P^*_t \quad.$$

For most of the period α, the share of total slaves who resided in rural areas was approximately .96. Therefore equation $(12')$ can be expressed as,

$$(17)\qquad Q^*_r = .025 - .05\,P^*_r \quad,$$

where $e_r = (1 - \alpha)e_t - [(1 - \alpha)/\alpha]e_c$, as per equation (13).

In the above derivation of the rural and the city demand functions, differences among the various P^*'s are ignored. This assumes that a weighted average of the prices of the different cities is fairly close to a weighted average of the rural prices. Most of the differences in the price series are probably due to heterogeneity in the labor input. The cities had more females whose prices were lower than males but fewer children and more highly skilled slaves. Each city had a different mix of these groups. This problem could have been corrected if there were many more observations and data series. Then an entire set of demand functions could have been constructed to account for elasticities of substitution less than infinity among groups of slaves. The present analysis has ignored differences among these price series.

Recall that the demand function for all slaves can be written in terms of the two sector demand curves as

$$(13) \qquad Q^*{}_t = [\alpha D^*{}_r + (1 - \alpha)D^*{}_c]$$
$$- [\alpha e_r + (1 - \alpha)e_c]P^* ,$$

and the corresponding supply function as

$$(18) \qquad Q^*{}_t = S^*{}_t + \gamma P^*{}_t ,$$

where γ is the elasticity of supply and $S^*{}_t$ measures, in rate-of-change form, the shift of the supply schedule. Therefore P^* can be expressed by

$$P^* = \frac{[\alpha D^*{}_r + (1 - \alpha)D^*{}_c] - S^*{}_t}{[\alpha e_r + (1 - \alpha)e_c] + \gamma}$$
$$= \frac{[\alpha D^*{}_r + (1 - \alpha)D^*{}_c] - S^*{}_t}{e_t + \gamma} .$$

As a first approximation set $\gamma = 0$, since it is very likely that γ was close to zero. This gives

$$(19) \qquad P^* = \frac{[\alpha D^*{}_r + (1 - \alpha)D^*{}_c] - Q^*{}_t}{e_t}$$
$$= \frac{D^*{}_t - Q^*{}_t}{e_t} .$$

Equation (19) shows how the competition between the rural and urban sectors contributed to the change in the price of slaves. Table 28 gives estimates for each of the four decades and for the entire forty-year period of the components of equation (19). The decade estimates for the shift parameters were computed using equation (3) and the slave labor force data underlying the regressions, table 27, part C. The decade estimates allow the shift term to differ from decade to decade instead of constraining it to be constant for the entire period. The assumption that the elasticities were constant from decade to decade is still employed, with $e_c = .86$, $e_r = .05$, and $e_t = .08$. The price series used in these computations was the weighted average of deflated rural Louisiana and Virginia data (see table 27, footnote a).

TABLE 28   Causes of the Cycles in Slave Prices, 1820–60

Decade (s)	$\alpha \overset{*}{D}_r$	$(1 - \alpha)\overset{*}{D}_c$	$\overset{*}{Q}_t = \overset{*}{S}_t$	$\overset{*}{D}_t - \overset{*}{Q}_t$	$\overset{}{e}_t$
1820–30	.025	.001	.027	-.001	.08
1830–40	.022	.003	.021	.004	.08
1840–50	.025	.000	.025	.000	.08
1850–60	.024	.002	.021	.005	.08
1820–60	.024	.001	.024	.001	.08

Source: See text. These data were computed using slave population data, the Virginia-Louisiana weighted prices, and the elasticity values $e_c = .86$, $e_r = .05$, $e_t = .08$.

For most of the period the cities had a minor, but not negligible, impact on the course of slave prices. During the period 1830–40, slave prices would have risen substantially less in the absence of the urban market, although the effect of the cities was much smaller in the other decades. The variation in the aggregate supply of slaves had a large impact on slave price movements during the period. Had the supply function, in rate-of-change form, remained constant, with the slave population growing at 2.4 percent a year, the price of slaves would have been steadier in its increase over time. The small cycles in $[D^*_t - Q^*_t]$ are magnified several times (twelvefold if $e_t = .08$) when they are divided by e_t. Therefore, the direction of slave-price movements over the decades is a direct consequence of the exogenous shifts in supply, although changes in demand were somewhat responsible. But the magnitude of these cycles results almost entirely from the small demand elasticity for the rural areas.

Although the cities and the rural areas were faced with similar price movements, the way in which they reacted to such price changes was quite different. This was due, in part, to differences in their elasticities of demand for slave labor. The cities, because of their larger elasticity of demand, had slave labor forces which were greatly affected by the large cycles in slave prices between 1820 and 1860. This can be seen from table 29, which gives

TABLE 29   Determinates of Q^*_c and Q^*_r, 1820–60

Decade(s)	$\overset{*}{D}_c$	$e_c\overset{*}{P}$	$\overset{*}{D}_r$	$e_r\overset{*}{P}$
1820-30	.023	-.001	.026	-.001
1830-40	.067	.040	.023	.002
1840-50	.005	-.008	.026	.000
1850-60	.033	.055	.025	.003
1820-60	.033	.020	.025	.001

Source: See text. Data used are those underlying table 28.

values for the terms in equations (11) $Q^*_c = D^*_c - e_cP^*$, and (12) $Q^*_r = D^*_r - e_rP^*$, by decade and for the entire period. In the urban sector, e_cP^* swamped or offset D^*_c. It swamped it in absolute magnitude in the last two decades and greatly offset it in the other years. Although the changes over time in D^*_c have not been fully explained in this chapter, variations in price combined with the large urban elasticity value were most important in determining the course of slavery in the cities. In the rural sector, however, e_rP^* was always much smaller than D^*_r. Variations in price for this labor market had little effect on the change in quantities, because the elasticity of demand was very small, $e_r = .05$.

This elasticity difference was crucial in determining the large changes which the cities experienced in their slave populations. Had this difference not existed, that is, had $e_c = e_r = e$, the demand functions for the two sectors during the entire period would have differed only by the intercept term.[18] Therefore, the cities would always have had slave populations which were growing at a rate greater than that of aggregate slave supply. Rather than declining between 1850 and 1860, slave populations would have been increasing at an average rate of 3.1 percent a year,[19] and the cycles which were observed in the rate of change of the urban slave population would have been reduced substantially.

The difference in the elasticities of demand for rural and urban slaves is thus the central factor in the relative decline of urban slavery during its last decade. Had these elasticities been identical, urban slavery would have appeared as "steady and vigorous" in its growth as did its rural counterpart. What, then, can account for this important difference in the elasticities of demand? Certainly the most important factor is the elasticity of substitution between slave labor and other productive inputs. The low rural elasticity of demand ($e_r = .05$) indicates that slave labor was a resource especially suited to Southern agriculture. It suggests that it was a factor for which there were few close substitutes.[20] The higher elasticity of demand for urban slave services ($e_c = .86$) indicates that slave labor, though it could be used and was desired in the cities, did not have the same special advantage in the cities that it had in the country. Free white and black labor in the cities was an especially good substitute for slave labor. Furthermore, urban slaves were producing more luxury items, the elasticity of demand for which was probably greater than that for agricultural staples.†

What made slaves so irreplaceable in the rural sector? The use of slaves in Southern agriculture appears to have enabled scale economies which would not have been achieved with free labor.[21] Although slave and free labor worked together on small farms, the labor force on large farms consisted almost exclusively of slaves. For reasons which are not yet entirely clear, free labor could not be mobilized for large-scale, gang labor on farms at a wage rate competitive with the shadow price on slaves.

There were no great economies in employing slave labor in urban industry, however. Living arrangements, as described in chapter 3, were generally made on an individual basis, indicating that there were no scale economies in providing food, housing, child care, and so on. There were also few cases where living in the proximity of work made the distinct economic difference it appears to have made on plantations. Cities reduced the costs of hiring slaves, and large urban slave users could therefore have had much smaller holdings on average than could plantation owners. This also served to mitigate any scale economies in using slave versus free labor. The urban factory made it as easy to organize white labor as it was to organize slave labor into large-scale production units. Furthermore, immigrants who moved to the Southern part of the United States were attracted to the urban areas in far greater numbers than to the rural communities.[22] Therefore,

---

†The elasticity of demand for labor is greater the larger the elasticity of demand for its output, the larger the elasticity of substitution between it and other inputs, and the larger the elasticity of supply of its substitutes.

the supply elasticity of alternative labor in the cities was probably higher than it was in the agricultural regions.

Had the price of slaves slowed down in its rate of increase, the cities as an aggregate would have begun to gain slaves again. Two economic historians have estimated that slave prices would have risen by 1.3 percent annually between 1860 and 1890 if slavery had not been abolished.[23] If the elasticity and shift parameters had been stable during this period, the values from equations (15) and (17) could be used to estimate the growth in the rural and urban slave populations. Urban slavery, far from disintegrating, would have increased at an annual rate of 2.4 percent, and this figure might be biased downward because no consideration has been given to the post-1850 growth of smaller towns.

The parameter estimates presented in table 27 show that, far from being zero, the demand for urban slaves grew steadily over the period. Not only was this rate of increase in the demand for urban slaves positive, it was also sufficiently high to surpass that for the rural region. Therefore, explanations for the decline of urban slavery which have relied on "push" factors are clearly wrong.

Instead of simply dismissing this argument, one should point out why so many historians came to the conclusion that slavery was incompatible with cities. These persons were misled by the urban slave population data. They assumed that a decreasing slave population and labor force implied a steadily declining demand for urban slaves. To explain what they perceived as a "pushing out" of slaves from the cities, they emphasized factors (such as those which could be included in the T variable) which might have resulted in a decreased demand for urban slaves. But they failed to take into account the full array of components influencing the course of the urban demand for slaves. Because they were too preoccupied with factors serving to decrease demand, they neglected the forces which stimulated it. Among these forces was the growth in the demand for the products produced by slaves, the rate of increase in the free population, and the possible rise, during some periods, in the price of free labor.

Although the urban sector demand function has a large shift term, some individual cities do not. Indeed, the regressions in table 27, part C, show that the inclusion of the rate of increase in the free population usually decreased the residual shift parameter, and for the cases of New Orleans, Louisville, and the New South aggregate the constant terms were negative after this additional variable was included. This demonstrates that market-size factors were important for most cities and appear to have dominated the other demand components for slaves.[24] Thus, it is conceivable that the special costs of maintaining slaves in an urban society were internalized, for a $\hat{D}'^* < 0$ indicates that some other factors influencing demand must have had a negative impact. One such factor stressed in historical literature has been T^*, the rate of increase in slave taxes, license fees, and so on. Although this implies that some factors not accounted for by Q^*_{fp} had a negative effect, it does not follow that the costs included in T dominated the course of demand. Furthermore, most of the cities and two urban aggregates had $\hat{D}'^* > \hat{D}^*$, showing that excluded factors had a powerful *positive* impact.

Even if these special urban costs did increase for some cities, equation (5) shows that such costs must have been a fairly large percentage of the annual hire rate to have affected demand noticeably. That is, ϕ or (T/P) must have been a large fraction for T^* to have affected Q^* in more than a trivial way. But the evidence marshaled in chapter 3 indicates that ϕ was very small, and T^* was not necessarily positive in the 1850s or, for that matter, during any but the early decades studied.

For T^* to have been a positive number, some of the costs that slaves have been viewed as imposing on urban society must have been shifted to slaveowners. Such internalization of costs may have taken place in several ways. Laws to control job holding and slave mobility may have been both passed and enforced. Prison and court costs, whether internalized directly through user charges or indirectly through taxation, would have been an additional influence on the demand for urban slaves. Harassment in the form of reduced employment due to jail sentences and lengthy court hearings would also be costs which reacted on demand. Moreover, the general feeling of the white populace about slaves and the possibility of slave insurrection was an influence on demand that is difficult to isolate and measure.

The regressions, combined with other evidence, suggest that these costs of slaveholding did not increase as rapidly as many have presumed—if, indeed, they increased at all. In addition, their magnitude was never very great, taken as a percentage of the annual value of a slave rental; that is, ϕ was small.

The background of the taxation process in the cities was presented in chapter 3, and a brief summary here will suffice to show that rules and fines were initiated early in urban slave history. Although it is possible that the enforcement of these laws was strengthened in the 1850s, no substantial evidence to support such a hypothesis has been found (see table 12). Almost all cities had taxes on slaves, but, as the Appendix shows, these were in general small and did not change very much over time. Only two cities, Savannah and Charleston, had substantial badge fees for slaves who hired their time or who were hired out. But these, too, were in effect early in these cities' histories and were not increased much through time. The highest badge fee was $10.56 for carpenters, tailors, and other skilled tradesmen in Savannah in 1839, which was lowered to $10 in 1854. The yearly net hire for such a skilled slave in 1854 was probably around $150 to $200, so that the badge fee was about 5 to 7 percent of the rental rate. This puts a lower bound on ϕ for skilled slaves in these cities. But it must be remembered that it is more important to measure how this fee changed through time. That is, T^* affects D^* directly (tempered by ϕ and ϵ), and it does not appear that T^* was positive in these cities during the crucial decade of the 1850s.

Another negative influence on D^* was the problem of runaway slaves. It is possible that some cities, especially those in border states, had small D^*'s because runaways increased over time, serving to dampen demand. As noted in chapter 3, the problem of runaways seems to have been a relatively greater one in the cities than in the rural community. But rural border areas probably suffered the same problem that the Border State cities faced, that of escape into free territory. One historian has claimed that Missouri suffered most severely, especially during the 1850s, from the loss of slaves because the "Underground Railway ran into the State from three sides, and its service appears to have been efficient."[25] That Saint Louis felt similar pressure is suggested by the fact that "in 1846 a mass-meeting of [her] citizens was held . . . 'to devise ways and means to protect their slave property.' "[26] Some Border State cities may have experienced real losses because of their proximity to freedom. Yet these losses must have been relatively very small, for the free black population of the North did not increase greatly between 1850 and 1860.

Differences among Southern Cities in the Course of Urbanization

Although the two-sector analysis has served to clarify much about the course of urban slavery, use of the disaggregated regression results sheds additional light concerning differences and similarities among various cities. Even though the average shift parameter for the cities was large and positive, some cities showed smaller increases and some larger changes in demand. The urban elasticities of demand also varied much from city to city. The descriptive history of the cities in chapter 2 suggested that each was subject to different economic forces. Expanding that view, this section explores fluctuations in the magnitude of the shift parameters among the four decades for the ten cities and attempts to explain the large cycles which each of the cities experienced in their slave populations. The reaction of each of the cities to the large fluctuations in slave prices tells much about the underlying economic factors in these urban areas.

Fluctuations in the Magnitude of D^*_i   The estimation of the elasticities of demand for urban slaves enables the calculation of the shift terms decade by decade, for each of the cities and for all slave states. The procedure is identical to that used in part 1 of this chapter but employs the computed elasticities rather than assumed values. These estimates are based on equation

(3) $D^*_i = Q^*_i + e_i P^*_i$.

In calculating the values of D^*_i, I have used what I regard as the best estimate of e for each city and for all slave states. These, which can be found in table 30, are from table 27, part C.

Table 31 shows how the demand for slaves varied among the four decades, assuming that the estimated price elasticity was constant over the entire forty-year period. One important conclusion which can be drawn from these data is that demand movements for urban slaves were continuously strong over this period. Only four of the forty urban observations indicate that demand was decreasing, and only one of these occurs during the 1850s. Many of the cities display a growth in demand greater than that of all slave states within the same decade. Two of the urban aggregates,

TABLE 30   Maximum Likelihood Demand Elasticity Estimates for Ten Cities, Three Urban Aggregates, and All Slave States

	$\hat{e}$		$\hat{e}$
All slave states	.08	Richmond	.12
Baltimore	1.38	Saint Louis	1.53
Charleston	.72	Savannah	.27
Louisville	.46	Washington	1.03
Mobile	.54	Old South cities	.92
New Orleans	.16	New South cities	.21
Norfolk	.81	Border State cities	1.78

Source: Table 27, part C.

TABLE 31   Estimates of D^* for Four Decades, Using the Maximum Likelihood Estimates of e

	1820–30	1830–40	1840–50	1850–60
All slave states	.024	.027	.028	.026
Baltimore	.030	.036	–.012	.031
Charleston	.006	.024	.024	.006
Louisville	.107	.051	.047	.009
Mobile	.039	.138	.039	.044
New Orleans	.015	.102	–.036	–.009
Norfolk	.030	.036	.019	.012
Richmond	.046	.030	.026	.026
Saint Louis	.050	–.008	.017	.034
Savannah	.027	.029	.031	.025
Washington	.046	.016	.017	.031
Old South cities	.042	.048	.025	.035
New South cities	.018	.106	–.020	.003
Border cities	.066	.063	.038	.056

Source: $D^* = Q^* + eP^*$, where Q^* is the rate of change in the slave labor force. P^* identical to that used in table 27, part C, for each city or region, and e is from table 30.

the Old South and Border State cities, maintained a rapid growth in demand, and in only one case, the Old South in 1840–50, was this less than that for all slave states. Although the New South cities exceeded the total in just one instance, they experienced negative growth in only one decade, 1840–50. This decade of declining demand followed one of exceptionally rapid increases. It is quite possible that the 1830–40 boom in this region was greater than had been desired, and that the 1840–50 decline reflects a readjustment. Certainly, an average of these two periods yields D^*'s much in line with the others in the table.

It is obvious from the data in table 31 that oscillations in the urban slave labor force were not the result only of continuously changing shift factors. It was not generally the case that these cities experienced a greater-than-average increase in demand for slaves during 1820–30 and 1840–50, those decades when equilibrium quantities expanded. In fact, 1840–50 was a period of a sluggish growth in urban slave demand, and 1830–40 appears as strong as 1820–30. The factors which did account for the cycles in the urban slave labor force will be taken up in the next section.

Not only was urban slave demand strong during the entire period; it also did not weaken for most cities during the last decade. All three urban aggregates experienced an increase in the rate at which demand expanded from 1840–50 to 1850–60. Although, in general, demand movements were greater in the beginning of this forty-year period than at the end, they were not noticeably so.

A sensitivity analysis was performed on these data (see table 32), for three values of e (.5, 1, 1.5) for the cities, and three others (.10, .25, .50)[27] for all slave states. This exercise shows that the estimates in table 31 are crucially dependent on the elasticity value for some decades, especially those in which price changes were large and could easily swamp changes in quantities. For example, a value of $e = .5$ is sufficient to produce a positive D^* for New Orleans, 1850–60, whereas the maximum likelihood estimate of $e = .16$ yielded a negative D^*. A value of $e = 1$ for the same city and decade yields a very large D^*. Since the computed elasticities, as discussed previously, are probably biased downward, this sensitivity analysis is helpful in ascertaining bounds on D^*. In general, the analysis in both tables 31 and 32 reveals an impressive growth in demand for all decades with the possible exception of 1840–50, when slave prices were declining rapidly. It

TABLE 32 Average Annual Rates of Growth in Demand for the Slave Labor Force in Ten Cities, Three Urban Aggregates, and All Slave States, Using Three Values of *e*

Decades	Old South Cities .5	1	1.5	New South Cities .5	1	1.5	Border State Cities .5	1	1.5	All Slave States .10	.25	.50
1850–60	.016	.039	.062	.022	.053	.085	-.003	.020	.043	.027	.037	.053
1840–50	.027	.025	.023	.028	-.044	-.058	.029	.027	.025	.028	.027	.025
1830–40	.030	.051	.073	.115	.129	.144	.008	.029	.051	.028	.035	.046
1820–30	.035	.044	.054	.019	.020	.022	.042	.051	.061	.024	.022	.020

Decades	Baltimore .5	1	1.5	Charleston .5	1	1.5	Louisville .5	1	1.5	Mobile .5	1	1.5
1850–60	-.009	.014	.037	-.006	.021	.048	.011	.034	.057	.042	.073	.105
1840–50	-.008	-.010	-.012	.027	.022	.018	.047	.045	.043	.040	.026	.012
1830–40	-.002	.020	.042	.017	.034	.051	.053	.074	.100	.137	.151	.166
1820–30	.014	.023	.033	.010	.002	-.006	.108	.117	.127	.039	.040	.042

Decades	New Orleans .5	1	1.5	Norfolk .5	1	1.5	Richmond .5	1	1.5	Saint Louis .5	1	1.5
1850–60	.013	.044	.076	-.004	.019	.042	.043	.066	.089	-.031	.001	.033
1840–50	-.045	-.060	-.074	.020	.018	.016	.024	.022	.020	-.046	.032	.018
1830–40	.112	.126	.141	.022	.043	.065	.047	.068	.090	-.038	-.023	-.009
1820–30	.017	.018	.020	.024	.033	.043	.054	.063	.073	.047	.048	.050

Decades	Savannah .5	1	1.5	Washington .5	1	1.5
1850–60	.032	.048	.064	.007	.030	.053
1840–50	.030	.027	.025	.019	.017	.015
1830–40	.043	.073	.103	.029	.015	.037
1820–30	.023	.013	.004	.036	.045	.055

Source: $D^* = Q^* + eP^*$, where Q^* = average annual rate of change in the slave labor force and all prices are identical to those used in table 27, part C.

appears that the cities did not gain sufficient numbers of slaves during that decade to indicate as large an increase in demand as the quantity data alone had previously signified.

The classification of Southern cities into the three categories— Old South, New South, and Border State—is used throughout this book, and some of the implications of these distinctions have become apparent in the empirical estimation of the model. An underlying assumption of the aggregated regressions in table 27 was that differences in the elasticity and shift parameter estimates among cities in any one aggregate were not as great as differences among cities in different aggregates.[28] This implies certain common characteristics among the cities in a particular region, and the individual city regressions tend to substantiate these distinctions. The Border State cities had the greatest elasticities of demand, the Old South the next greatest, and the New South cities the lowest.

Although I have distinguished among Southern cities by a commonly used regional breakdown, the characteristics attributed to them have not been as traditional. The qualities stressed in chapters 2, 3, and 4 as common to the Border State cities were (1) large and rapidly expanding free populations, (2) a higher-than-average percentage of the free population that was foreign born, and (3) slave populations with an increasing female-to-male ratio and an older-than-average mean age. More traditional characteristics of the Border State cities might encompass political and social differences from the cities further south. By avoiding these distinctions one can discover how the shifts in urban slave labor can be accounted for by more basic economic factors.[29]

It appears from the regression analysis that the very large oscillations in slave labor quantities experienced in the Border State cities can be explained more by economic factors bearing on the substitutability of slave for free labor than by a changing political and social climate. The loss of slave labor which many Southern cities experienced during the 1850s seems less the result of strong antislave forces in the cities than the consequence of an increased free population which was a substitute for male slave labor. Female slaves, whose skills appear more specific to individual households and whose labor was less substitutable for that of white women, remained in the cities. The aging of the slave labor force in these areas also fits into this general explanation, for older slaves would have had more specific skills than those who were younger.

The two New South cities, Mobile and New Orleans, were lumped together because they were both influenced by the delta commerce. They both experienced a rapid expansion in slave populations and in the demand for slaves during 1830–40, a period in which the New South, in general, grew quite rapidly.

What have traditionally been grouped together as Old South cities include a far more diverse group than the other classifications, although they too had certain common characteristics. In general, these cities had (1) slave populations which were a fairly large percentage of their total population, (2) a rather equal number of female and male slaves, (3) large numbers of skilled male slaves, and (4) a smaller nonnative percentage than the other regions.

But differences among these cities are also apparent. Richmond stands out as the city with the most stable and largest increases in slave labor demand. It is also the city with one of the smaller elasticities of demand. Richmond was the most industrial of all the urban areas, and it was not subject to as large an influx of immigrants as were most other cities. Therefore, Richmond's slaves had few substitutes, and they were, on average, a more skilled group than were found in the other cities. These facts can account for the low elasticity value ($\hat{e} = .12$) for Richmond slaves. Charleston, on the other hand, decreased in importance as a port during the 1850s. This may account for some of the sluggish growth in demand for Charleston slaves during that period. Savannah grew at a steadier pace, similar to Richmond's, and this is reflected in the growth of the demand for slaves in that city.

Although my analysis has stressed economic factors in determining changes in the equilibrium quantities of slaves, I do not mean to imply that social and political explanations are unworthy. The limited number of data points prevented a more thorough and rigorous model which could explore these factors. For example, the number of immigrants each city received may well have been a function of the political climate in that region. It may also have been a function of the percentage of the urban citizenry which was slave, and not dependent only on the wage rate. But this analysis has shown that, whatever the omitted factors, they appear less important in analyzing the broad changes in urban slave populations than the few economic variables specified in the model. Further, as shown in the next section, the large oscillations in slave labor can be easily rationalized within this simple model, and one need not look to changing social and political factors in the cities. Exogenous forces, in the form of slave price changes, determined far more by rural than by urban factors (see table 28), explain to a large degree the urban slave labor oscillations.

The Cycles in the Urban Slave Labor Force

It was pointed out in chapter 4 that (1) there were large cycles in the deflated price and hire rate data for slaves, with these prices rising rapidly during the decades of the 1830s and the 1850s, and declining or rising very slightly during the 1820s and 1840s; (2) there were large cycles in the cities' slave labor forces, and the decades in which the urban slave labor forces grew the most were those in which prices rose the least; and (3) the total United States slave labor force also displayed some cyclical behavior, but these oscillations were much smaller than the pronounced urban swings.

The process which produced the large price and hire rate cycles has been described. It has also been shown that, given these changes in price, the cities, because of larger demand elasticities, reacted more violently than did rural regions. The elasticity differences seemed to account for many of the strange population and labor force cycles noted in chapter 4. The shift terms by decade for the cities, assuming constant elasticities, tended to offset some of these oscillations. It appears that changing shift factors alone cannot account for the changing slave quantities. I now explore the extent to which differences in the price elasticities of demand account for these cycles. First I shall deal with differences between the cities and the aggregate slave state figures, and then I shall attempt to account for differences among the various cities.

To address the first of these issues, that is, the differences between the cities and the total figures, write equation (2) for a particular city and equation (8) for all slave states:

(2) $Q^*{}_i = D^*{}_i - e_i P^*{}_i$,

(8) $Q^*{}_t = D^*{}_t - e_t P^*{}_t$.

Subtracting one of these equations from the other yields:

(20) $(Q^*_i - Q^*_t) = (D^*_i - D^*_t)$

$- [e_t (P^*_i - P^*_t)]$

$- [P^*_i (e_i - e_t)]$.

Thus, there are three reasons why the movements of the slave labor forces in urban and all areas, Q^*_i and Q^*_t, may have differed:

1. Demand need not have grown at the same rate in the city and the aggregate, that is, D^*_i may have been different from D^*_t.

2. The slave price movements may not have been the same, that is, P^*_i may have been different from P^*_t. This could have occurred for a variety of reasons. Short-run fluctuations of supply and demand in a city may have resulted in price movements slightly different from those in rural areas. In addition, any region's price will equalize with any other only to the extent that it does not pay to transport a slave from one area to the next. Therefore, prices may not be identical even in equilibrium, although the difference in the prices cannot exceed the transport and transactions costs. The prices will thus fall between two bounds which depend on the cost of transacting.

3. The elasticity of demand may not have been the same between the city and the aggregate, that is, $e_i \neq e_t$.

Table 33 shows for each city and decade the estimate of $(D^*_i - D^*_t)$ from table 31 and the values of $[-e_t (P^*_i - P^*_t)]$, and $[-P^*_i(e_i - e_t)]$, that is, the three parts of equation (20). It is obvious that differences in price, when multiplied by e_t, are not an important feature of this explanation. The price movements among all regions were very similar (see table 23), and multiplication by $e_t = .08$ further reduces the importance of this factor. Therefore, the crucial features of a rationalization of these cycles are, using the column numbers of table 33, (1) $(D^*_i - D^*_t)$, and $(3)[-P^*_i(e_i - e_t)]$. In general, the higher the e_i the more the last column (3) in table 33 explains differences in the rate of growth in the labor force. The smaller the e_i, the more the first column (1) explains these variations. As noted earlier, there is reason to

TABLE 33 Three Explanations for Differences in Q^*_i and Q^*_t, Using Equation (20), for Ten Cities over Four Decades

City	$D^*_i - D^*_t$ (1)				$-e_t(P^*_i - P^*_t)$ (2)				$-P^*_i(e_i - e_t)$ (3)			
	1820–1830	1830–1840	1840–1850	1850–1860	1820–1830	1830–1840	1840–1850	1850–1860	1820–1830	1830–1840	1840–1850	1850–1860
Baltimore	.006	.009	-.040	.005	.002	.000	.000	-.001	-.025	-.056	.005	-.060
Charleston	-.018	-.003	-.004	-.020	.000	-.001	.000	-.001	.010	-.022	.006	-.035
Louisville	.083	.024	.019	-.017	.002	.000	.000	-.001	-.007	-.016	.002	-.017
Mobile	.015	.111	.011	.018	.001	.000	-.002	.000	-.001	-.013	.013	-.029
New Orleans	-.009	.075	-.064	-.035	.001	.000	-.002	.000	.000	-.002	.002	-.005
Norfolk	.006	.009	-.009	-.014	.002	.000	.000	-.001	-.014	-.033	.003	-.035
Richmond	.022	.003	-.002	.000	.002	.000	.000	-.001	-.001	-.002	.000	-.002
Saint Louis	.026	-.035	-.011	.008	.001	.000	-.002	.000	-.004	-.042	.041	-.091
Savannah	.003	.002	.003	-.001	-.001	.001	.000	-.003	.004	-.011	.001	-.006
Washington	.022	-.011	-.011	.005	.002	.000	.000	-.001	-.018	-.041	.004	-.044

Sources: D^*_i and D^*_t are from table 31; $\hat{e}_i$ and $\hat{e}_t$ are from table 30; P^*_t is a weighted average of rural Louisiana and Virginia deflated prices; P^*_i for each city is that used for the regressions in table 27, part C.

believe that some of the elasticities are biased downward. The elasticities computed in table 27, part C, and given in table 30 have been used, and for some cities these are very small. This is especially true of New Orleans; differences in the shift terms explain almost all of the difference in the rate of change in that city's quantities. For other cities, the difference in the elasticities, that is column (3), accounts for much of the difference between Q^*_i and Q^*_t. This is especially true of Baltimore.

There are some cities for which numbers are large in both columns (1) and (3). Saint Louis is one city for which columns (1) and (3) have large entries. Here the differences in the shift terms create some cyclical behavior, which is sometimes accentuated, sometimes moderated, by differences in the elasticities. The result is that the growth in Saint Louis's slave labor force oscillated tremendously around that for the aggregate, which was much steadier in its growth. In the case of Charleston, column (1) is always negative, indicating that the growth in Charleston's slave demand was always less than the aggregate. Despite this there were large cycles in its slave quantities caused by the factors in column (3). Charleston's price elasticity of demand was sufficiently larger than that for all slave states to accentuate the price changes. This was reinforced by (1) in two decades but swamped (1) in the other two.

Some part of the slave labor force oscillations, however, resulted from varying shift factors and did not entirely originate in elasticity differences. Data limitations have prevented a thorough researching of the components of this factor, although some evidence has been given to explain the experience of a few cities.

Fig. 5 explains graphically how elasticity differences between urban and aggregate demand functions could cause very large changes in the urban quantities. The D^*_i function drawn is for Savannah, and that labeled D^*_t is for all slave states. The intercept and elasticity data for both functions were taken from table 27, part A. The two lines labeled $S^*_{1830-1840}$ and $S^*_{1840-1850}$ are slave supply functions in growth rate terms for these decades, under the assumption made previously that the aggregate supply elasticity (γ) for slave labor services was zero.

The graph demonstrates the model under the assumption that the shift parameter was constant ($\hat{D}^*_i = .28$ and $\hat{D}^*_t = .27$) over the four decades. Savannah's slave labor force underwent larger

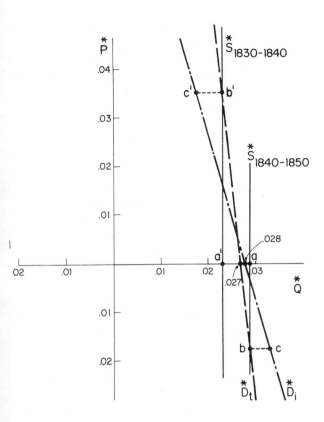

Figure 5. A Graphical Representation of the Model: Savannah and All Slave States (see table 27, part A)

changes than the total because the elasticity of demand for Savannah slaves was higher ($\hat{e}_i = .274$) than that for all slave states ($\hat{e}_t = .095$).[30] If, for explanatory purposes, it is assumed that the price changes used for both Savannah and the aggregate were the same, then one can determine a unique equilibrium in this model. The market clearing change in prices is given by the intersection of S^* and $D^*{}_t$. For the 1830s this is measured by the distance $a'b'$ and for the 1840s by ab. Given this change in prices, the city $Q^*{}_i$ can be read off the $D^*{}_i$ schedule. In this example, Savannah had a $Q^*{}_i$ which was less than $Q^*{}_t = S^*$ by $c'b'$ for 1830–40. It was greater than $Q^*{}_t = S^*$ by bc in 1840–50.

The rural demand schedule has not been drawn, but the graph contains almost enough information to construct it. Recall from equation (13) that the rural shift term and elasticity are convex combinations of those for the cities and the aggregate. Given the proper weight, that is, the share of slaves which was urban, the rural demand function can be determined. It is obvious that the growth in the rural slave labor force exceeded that for the aggregate during the 1830s and was less than the aggregate during the 1840s.

Because the city had a larger demand elasticity, it reacted more sharply to changes in price. During the 1830s Savannah's slave labor force grew far less rapidly than that of the aggregate, but during the 1840s falling slave prices led urban buyers and hirers to switch from other productive inputs to slaves. The greater substitution possibilities in the cities seem to account for much of the variability in slave quantities. Had another city with a larger elasticity been drawn (e.g., Washington), the labor force cycles would have been more extreme. In some cases the very large price increases of the 1830s and 1850s led a substantial number of urban owners and hirers to switch out of slave labor. This substitution was so great that for some cities the slave labor force declined during these decades.

One of the most important results of this research is the finding that the period of the 1850s was not unique. It was but a small part of a forty-year period during which there was great variability in many factors bearing on urban slavery. Viewing the 1850s in this light, one can no longer interpret declining slave quantities during that decade as signaling the demise of urban slavery.

Returning to table 33 to separate the effects of the shift terms and the elasticities by decade, it is obvious that the cyclical nature of, for example, Savannah's slave labor force was almost entirely caused by differences in the elasticities, the term in column (3). The shift term mildly accentuated these cycles in all but one decade. Taking a less clear example, that of New Orleans, leads to slightly different conclusions. The elasticity effect in this case, that is, column (3), results in very small cycles. But the shift term given in column (1) swamps the negative entry in (3) for the 1830s. The result is not as simple as the Savannah case. Part of the change in New Orleans's slave labor force was due to variations in the shift term over the decades. Had this not been changing, the elasticity effect would have yielded cycles similar to those observed for many of the other cities.

It is also interesting to observe how the cycles in the urban slave labor forces differed among the cities. This problem can be analyzed in much the same way as that which compared each city to the aggregate. Write equation (2) for two cities, 1 and 2:

(2′) $Q^*_1 = D^*_1 - e_1 P^*_1$,

(2″) $Q^*_2 = D^*_2 - e_2 P^*_2$.

Subtracting (2″) from (2′) yields:

$$(21) \qquad (Q^*_1 - Q^*_2) = (D^*_1 - D^*_2)$$
$$- [e_1 (P^*_1 - P^*_2)]$$
$$- [P^*_2 (e_1 - e_2)] \ .$$

As in the preceding analysis, differences in the growth of the slave labor force between any two cities can be explained by (1) differences in the rate at which demand grew, (2) differences in slave price movements, (3) differences in the elasticity of demand for slave services between the two cities.

To illustrate this, two cities have been chosen: Washington (city 1) and Savannah (city 2). Of these, Washington underwent far more severe slave labor fluctuations than those experienced by Savannah. The slave price movements are not the same for these cities, but the column (2) figures are again small in comparison to those in (1) and (3). The figures below in table 34 for $[D^*_1 - D^*_2]$ and $[-P^*_2 (e_1 - e_2)]$ show that the difference

TABLE 34   A Comparison of Savannah and Washington Slave Cycles

$\overset{*}{D}_1 - \overset{*}{D}_2$				$-e_1(\overset{*}{P}_1 - \overset{*}{P}_2)$				$-\overset{*}{P}_2(e_1 - e_2)$			
820–830	1830–1840	1840–1850	1850–1860	1820–1830	1830–1840	1840–1850	1850–1860	1820–1830	1830–1840	1840–1850	1850–1860
(1)				(2)				(3)			
.019	+.013	+.014	−.006	+.010	−.005	.000	+.004	−.014	−.033	+.003	−.035

Source: See source note to table 33.

in the shift terms is somewhat responsible for the difference in the slave labor fluctuations. But the elasticity term was far more responsible for the fact that Washington's slave labor fluctuations were greater than Savannah's.

There are a priori reasons to expect certain cities to have had larger demand elasticities than others. Cities in which slaves were less skilled, especially those having fewer slaves with specific skills, would have the greatest elasticities. The same would be true for areas in which the elasticity of supply for alternative labor were large and in which technical substitution possibilities were great. These hypotheses seem to have been borne out in this study. The Border State cities of Baltimore, Saint Louis, and Washington have the highest elasticities. These were cities which received large numbers of foreign immigrants, as well as having substantial native-born laborers. Richmond and Savannah, which have lower elasticities, were cities in which slaves were employed by industry in large holdings and in which there appear to have been fewer substitutes for slave labor.

Those cities which had the highest elasticities of demand reacted most violently to the large changes in the price of slaves. In addition, within every city various slave subgroups had different elasticities of demand from one another. The labor input was not the homogeneous factor assumed in this study, and the more skilled probably had lower elasticities than those who were unskilled. Therefore, during these periods of slave labor oscillations the unskilled should have been experiencing even greater cycles than the skilled, which appears to have been the case. Some evidence noted in chapter 4 indicates that during the 1850s, when slaves were being "pulled" out of the cities, the more skilled slaves were retained and the less skilled were sold to rural areas.

6   Concluding Remarks

The main conclusion of this monograph is that slavery and Southern cities were not incompatible during the period 1820–60. Although there were some forces unique to urban areas which created an inhospitable environment for slavery, they were relatively weak. The additional costs that were imposed on urban owners and hirers amounted to only a small percentage of the yearly hire rate and do not appear to have increased over time. The index for the vigor of urban slavery which has been used in this study—the growth in the demand for urban slave services—appears to have been strong. Demand was growing faster in the urban than in the rural region. Moreover, urban demand was growing faster than the supply of slaves, which added a small fraction to the rise in slave prices during the period.

But to state that demand for urban slaves was rising during this period does not imply that all the determinants of demand contributed to this growth. The principal variable which stimulated the demand for city slaves was the growth in the urban market. In some cities, the rapid increase in their free populations as well as in their per-capita incomes enlarged the market for slave services. There were, however, forces which tended to decrease the demand for slaves. In two out of the ten cities studied, these forces were sufficiently strong to offset the effect of growth in market size.[1] But even here the most important of these forces was not the increase in costs specific to maintaining urban slaves. The issue of control raised in the traditional literature was clearly not important in impeding the progress of urban slavery. The evidence suggests that the decline in the price of free relative to slave labor was a major factor in restraining the growth in the demand for urban slaves.[2] It appears that immigrant labor, which settled in most of the Border State cities and in New Orleans, served to depress the relative price of free labor.

The various and conflicting economic forces in the cities led to variations in the growth of demand among the cities and the decades. Richmond, Louisville, Mobile, Savannah, and Washington showed the largest and most sustained increases in demand. Although the remaining cities displayed negative rates of growth during some decades, all but Baltimore had, on average, net increases in demand during the forty-year period. The rural demand for slaves increased steadily over these years. However, its average rate of growth was a little lower than that for the constructed, aggregate urban area.

The total demand for slaves in both the urban and rural markets was growing faster than or at an equal rate to supply for all but the first decade (see table 28). Movements in supply and demand, coupled with the small total demand elasticity for slave labor, produced large cycles in slave prices. The cities and the rural areas reacted quite differently to these price fluctuations. The highly elastic urban demand caused the city slave populations to be very sensitive to even small price changes. In certain decades, when the price of slaves was rising dramatically, increases in the demand for urban slaves were largely offset by the magnitude of the urban price elasticity. The 1850s were one such period of rising slave prices and hire rates. It was a combination of the large elasticity values and the increase in the price of slave labor which served to draw slaves out of the cities during that period. This movement did not signal the demise of the urban slavery. It was far more a function of the availability of low-cost substitute labor than of the inability to control urban slaves.

Slave labor was not the only group drawn from the cities during the 1850s. The free black population, as well, experienced rather small rates of increase. It is possible that the same forces which "pulled" slaves from urban employments also enticed free blacks into agricultural activities and into the smaller towns. Free blacks may have been "pushed" out of the cities to some extent as well. As we saw in chapter 3, many cities passed legislation to prohibit or limit the mobility of free blacks into various occupations.

The greatest part of the explanation for the rise in slave prices lies in the rural area's growth. The rising demand for urban slaves explains only a small part of the change in slave prices. Most of the price rise was ultimately generated by the rapid increase in the world demand for the products of Southern agriculture. As a consequence, slaves were pulled out of the urban areas by the increase in the demand for Southern agricultural staples.

Given the large oscillations in price among the various decades, the difference in the elasticities of demand for the city versus the rural areas determined the distribution of slaves. In certain decades the cities lost a considerable portion of their slave populations; in others, the cities bought and hired slaves from the rural areas. It is the elasticity difference (the urban elasticity was seventeen times that for the rural areas) that provides the key to these large population swings. One therefore needs an explanation for the high urban and the low rural elasticities.

The low rural elasticity indicates that there were few substitutes for slave labor in agriculture. That is, slaves were especially well suited for staple crop production. The high urban elasticity suggests that there were more and closer substitutes for slaves in urban activities but does not imply anything about the usefulness or desirability of slaves in the cities. The full reasons for slave labor's special efficiency in agriculture lie beyond the scope of this study. Current research, however, indicates that the slave form of labor enabled scale economies to be achieved in agriculture which were not possible with free labor.[3] Large-scale farms which employed the great majority of slave labor were more efficient than small ones. In addition, the average size of rural slaveholdings tripled between 1790 and 1860, which suggests that larger farms became even more efficient over time.

Urban slaves, on the other hand, were employed in a variety of activities for which scale economies were not important or were not specific to the slave organization of labor. Domestic service, for instance, did not involve economies of large scale. Urban factories and employment agencies appear to have been the only organizational devices through which urban industry could have reaped the benefits of economies of scale. But both do not appear to have been more efficient in the use of slave than free labor. The use of slave labor appears to have had little effect on productive efficiency in the cities.

It may appear that this discussion has brought us back to the traditional interpretation of the decline of urban slavery. This is not the case. Although prior arguments have suggested that slavery had a special advantage in rural areas, these varied theses, summarized in chapter 1, have also claimed that it was harder to control slaves in the cities and that bondsmen could not cope with factory work. The evidence presented here discredits that reasoning. The real problem of control which the ruling classes experienced did not concern slaves in cities but free labor in agriculture. While free laborers and slaves could be organized into relatively large-scale organizations in the cities, only slaves could be forced to work in the large-scale farms at prevailing wages and under the existing institutional arrangements.

It is very different to claim that the cities provided a hostile environment for slavery and that slavery had a comparative advantage in agricultural production. The former implies that the process of urbanization served to lower the profitability of slavery. The latter implies the cities' retention or rejection of slaves depended primarily on the price of alternative labor and the growth in the demand for Southern agricultural products. It follows that, in the absence of emancipation, the drain of slaves from the cities might not have continued. As Southern cities grew relative to the rural areas, and as the rate of growth in world demand for cotton waned after 1870, the cities would probably have gained slaves again.[4] The rate of increase in the price of slaves would have been moderated, and, if the price of free labor had remained constant, the cities would have found it profitable to substitute slave for free. The growth in cities after 1865 would have stimulated the demand for urban slaves through the market-size variable. The direction of the flow of slave labor from the cities to the country might well have been substantially reversed had emancipation not occurred.

Although I contend that urban slavery would have expanded in the hypothetical world of no emancipation, I do not believe that slavery would have survived indefinitely. My book, coupled with those on other aspects of slavery such as *Time on the Cross*, has shown that there were no inherent forces in the slave system causing it to decline. This does not imply that there would have been no contradictions in a more modern era. Few can imagine American black slavery surviving in an advanced industrial economy. Modern transportation networks, increased education, and industrial growth would all have led to its downfall. But the antebellum Southern cities analyzed in this book were not the large, industrial, cosmopolitan areas to which we are accustomed.

The large movements of slave labor from the cities to the country show the effectiveness with which the slave economy achieved labor transfers. These movements appear to have been rather intricate. Urban areas retained slaves with special urban skills during periods of rising rural prices while releasing those whose skills could be used with greater advantage in rural areas. Differences in the elasticities of demand among the cities suggest that slaves were used in various capacities and that different substitutes were available. Such differences in elasticity as well as those in the growth of demand led to considerable variation in the rate at which the cities individually released (or took in) slaves from the rural areas.

Far from being a rigid economic system, slavery was extremely flexible—most apparently so in the cities. During the forty-year period studied, many institutions developed which were more closely linked to urban than rural slavery. Hiring out, including the hiring out of their own time by slaves themselves, became widespread in almost all Southern cities, and it was also common for slaves to live apart from their owners.

Many have claimed that these freedoms heralded the demise of the slave system. There is no doubt that these added freedoms created certain new problems, but the problems were limited in scope and were controlled at quite moderate costs. The most striking feature of the urban experience was the capacity of slavery to adapt to a wide variety of special conditions. Adaptability made slavery more profitable in urban areas than it would otherwise have been and contributed to the rapid growth in the demand for slaves in the South.

I do not mean to suggest, of course, that urban slavery was a good institution benefiting both slave and master. On the contrary, I have indicated that the ruling class in Southern cities had the ability to subjugate people, even in work which was not predominantly agricultural. To do so and earn a profit, they had to yield to certain pressures and permit certain freedoms. But they also had to ensure that these freedoms were not used to undermine the system.

There appear to be two conflicting opinions concerning the freedoms given to urban slaves. One is that the less harsh environment placated slaves and made rebellion less probable. The other is that these freedoms were actual or potential weapons against the system and, hence, that fears of insurrection were warranted. I have suggested a third view: that slavery was adapted to the urban milieu. There were freedoms, but there was also a "web of restraints," to use Wade's phrase. Most writers have concluded that slavery and cities were incompatible because these researchers did not explore all aspects of urban slavery or analyze its changes during an extensive time period. They therefore turned to the peculiarities of urban slavery for a rationalization of their findings. In attempting to investigate this topic as thoroughly as possible, I hope I have also shed light on other aspects of American slave history that are, perhaps, even more interesting than the controversy I sought to resolve.

Epilogue

Slaves in urban areas appear to have been a more highly trained labor force than slaves working in agriculture. This was to be expected, for city work demanded more skills than did farming, and slavery gave an impetus to investment in such training. What became of these skills after 1865? Were they, in some sense, beneficial legacies of urban slavery?

Occupational data from the 1890 federal census point to a high level of black skill in Southern relative to Northern cities.[1] The skills that are especially prominent are, in fact, exactly those skills accumulated by urban slaves. They were passed on from generation to generation and remained even as late as 1890. Certain more modern trades were closed to blacks in both the North and the South, although entry to these trades appears to have been on a more discriminatory basis in the North. It seems that blacks could not get training in the newer methods of building and that the trades stemming from more recent technologies fostered stronger unions which excluded them. Furthermore, even though Southern blacks retained a fairly high level of skill by 1890, this level soon declined. Unions, some claim, became stronger, making headway in the traditionally unorganized South.[2]

The 1890 census lists occupation by race and sex for various cities—data in which the legacy of urban slavery can be discerned. In Charleston, which had a large number of slaves in the antebellum period and was more than half black in 1890, 24 percent of black males over the age of ten listed their occupations as artisans, skilled tradesmen, and mechanics.[3] But only 18 percent of white males in the same city listed their employment as such. In Richmond, these figures are 14 percent for blacks and 28 percent for whites, and in New Orleans 17 percent for blacks and 22 percent for whites. But in the Northern cities of New York and Philadelphia the equivalent data display a very low level of black skill. Only 3 percent of New York's blacks had mechanical and trade positions, but 31 percent of the whites did. In Philadelphia these figures are 8 percent for blacks and 31 percent for whites.

Thus it appears that much of the skill differential between the North and the South is a legacy of slavery. Trades were passed on in the postbellum South from father to son and from tradesmen to helpers.

But another, somewhat complementary, explanation for these data could also be correct. Part of the observed differential might be due to discrimination in the purchasing of goods and services. To the extent that the black community was large and not very dispersed geographically, sufficient demand could be generated to maintain a substantial level of skill among blacks.[4] Therefore differences among the three Southern cities mentioned above could be explained by the fact that 56 percent of Charleston's population was black in 1890, as against only 27 percent of New Orleans's and 40 percent of Richmond's. The wide gap between black skills in the South and those in Philadelphia and New York might be explained by the fact that only 2 percent of New York's and 4 percent of Philadelphia's populations were black. But these latter groups may not have been highly dispersed geographically.

Additional evidence on how much freedmen's skills were a function of their training under slavery can be found by looking at individual occupations. Carpentry was an occupation for which many slaves were trained. Indeed, almost half of Charleston's carpenters in 1848 were slaves and 54 percent were black.[5] By 1890 this figure was 76 percent, although only 8.4 percent of New York's blacks would have been carpenters, had its labor force had the same racial composition as Charleston's in 1890.[6] Although blacks were well represented in carpentry in the South, they were not numerous in the machinist category in either the North or the South. This suggests that blacks were excluded from more modern, skilled occupations in both the North and the South but retained older skills in the South.

These data must be interpreted cautiously, for skill differentials can be fully explained only with a more elaborate model of the postbellum occupational structure. Secondary literature, however, substantiates the hypothesis that slavery had a large impact on postbellum skill levels. Frederick Douglass claimed that trades were cut off to northern blacks in 1870 but that "the South offered the greatest opportunities, for all trades [in the early seventies] were shut against the Negro in the North. In the South . . . the Negroes could be carpenters, blacksmiths, shoemakers, bricklayers, shipwrights, joiners, and in some places teachers, preachers, lawyers, doctors, clerks and hotelkeepers."[7]

Unfortunately, even the South did not extend job opportunities to blacks for long. "Certain significant forces at work between 1890 and 1910 caused a decline in the relative importance of Negro industrial workers classified as mechanics and artisans."[8] Although this was true for both the South and the North, it was more noticeable in the South, where blacks had long been in control of many of the skilled trades.

There are two reasons for this dramatic change in the South. DuBois and Dill, discussing one reason in their study of the black artisan, contend that "the new industrial development of the South made new demands upon the mechanic. Old methods of production gave way to new ones and the Negro mechanic, schooled in the economy of the ante-bellum days and knowing so little of mills and machinery, found himself unprepared to meet the demands of the new economy."[9] A related explanation for the decline of the Southern black artisan was the expansion of unions from the North to the South. This is not meant to imply that Northerners had a greater penchant for discrimination but that economic and other factors made early unionization stronger in the North. Unionization and other concerted efforts appear to have been necessary to enforce discrimination, because there were always incentives for competitive persons to "cheat" by employing blacks and purchasing their goods and services.[10] Of course there were other, more violent means of effecting discrimination. But, according to Charles Wesley, trade unions gave blacks the "greatest troubles. . . . The impulse to the unionization of the South was first given by migrating workers who speedily united in organizations such as they had been accustomed to in the North. The American Federation of Labor also sent its agents into the South to accelerate the movement."[11] Wesley cites unions in Atlanta, Baltimore, Louisville, and Washington as effectively closing trades to blacks. Trades like carpentry and painting, which had traditionally been occupations held by blacks, were now available only to whites.

Chapter 3 stressed that urban slavery led to the training of blacks in many occupations and that this training and its associated freedoms did not lead to the decline of urban slavery. But the positive impact of slavery on postbellum black skills in the South does not imply that slavery was a good institution. Black skill levels were suppressed in the North because of discrimination, and the same discrimination held the Southern black in bondage. Without that bondage, education levels must certainly have been even higher. The skill differences only indicate that under slavery blacks were trained because owners protected their investments from the concerted efforts of white artisans and mechanics. When Southern industrialization modernized the skilled work performed by blacks in the building trades, labor unions, at first only powerful in the North, also became an effective means of discrimination in the South, and new training was denied to many blacks. Surprising as it may seem, slavery was not solely responsible for the low level of black skill in early twentieth-century America.

Appendix

Timetable of
City Ordinances
Relating to Slavery

This list of ordinances is not comprehensive, for some records are not extant and others could not be located in archives. In addition, only those ordinances considered to be important have been listed. Those regulating, for example, the local slave markets and social behavior have been omitted. The wording used, in most instances, has been taken directly from the original source, and in other cases a brief summary has been given. Penalties have not been listed. In most cases the date given is the year in which the original ordinance was passed, but where none was listed the publication date of the ordinance book was used. For sources, see the Bibliography, Archival Material.

Charleston

Year

1800   Assemblages of slaves, even with white persons, in a confined or secret place, and assemblages after dark are unlawful.

1806   Slaves are not to occupy houses without tickets from their owners and it is not lawful to hire directly to a slave any lot, house or enclosure.

        Slaves are not to carry on any mechanic or handicraft trade for their direct personal benefit. No person shall put a slave as an apprentice in any mechanic or handicraft trade under the charge of another slave.

        Slaves are not to buy, sell or trade goods, with the exception that slaves can sell meat, fruit and vegetables with a ticket, and milk, grain, fruit and other goods sent from their owners' plantation without a ticket.

        No one is to employ slaves in shops, unless in the presence of a white person.

Badges must be obtained for slaves who are hired out, and these slaves must be registered with the City Treasurer. [See 1843 for badge fee schedule.]

1830 Mechanics are not required to take out badges for Negroes hired to persons carrying on the same business as themselves.

1832 $1.50 tax for every slave, $3.00 each above 10 slaves, and $5.00 for over 20 slaves, except for those belonging to mechanics.

1837 Minimum wages set for slave porters and day laborers at $1.00 for a full day's labor.

1839 Slaves can be sold liquor with a ticket from their owner.

1843 Badges for hired slaves are to be purchased in January for one year. Price schedule (with 1806 prices shown for comparison):

	1843	1806
Handicraft tradesman	$7	$3
Carter, drayman, porter, or day laborer	4	2
Fisherman	4	1
Fisherwoman	2	1
House servant or washerwoman	2	1
Seller of fruits or cakes	5	15

(reduced to $5 in 1813)

1845 Every slave taxed $2.50.

1846 Slaves under 12 years old are taxed $1.25; those above and equal to 12 years old are taxed $2.00.

1847 Revises above by increasing tax from $2.00 to $2.50.

1848 All slaves taxed $2.25, regardless of age.

Negroes or slaves must obtain badges to work for other Negroes or slaves.

1850 All slaves taxed $3.00.

1851 Revises above to $2.50.

1855–
1859 Tax on slaves set at $3.00 for all.

Mobile

1826   Trading with slaves is prohibited, except with permission of owners or employers.

Slaves who hire their own time by the day must be registered in the Mayor's Office and obtain a badge (no fee), which must be worn.

Slaves authorized to be hired by the day must hire their time from specially appointed stands in the city.

1828   Self hiring and hiring without the consent of one's master are illegal.

1831   Assemblage by more than four slaves is illegal.

1843   Badges for hiring are $1.00.

Slaves are not to reside apart from their owners without a permit from the clerk of the city and a posting of $100 bond for each grown slave who lives out.

1858   Slaves who work for their owner but who live in separate lodgings may do so if their owner files a record about this with the city clerk and pays $1.00.

Slaves cannot hire their own time or the time of other slaves.

No person shall permit a slave to hire out his own time by the day, unless he has recorded the name, age, and sex of the slave with the city clerk's office and purchased a badge for $5.00.

Any slave brought into the city for sale or hire is taxed $1.00.

New Orleans

1817   No slave may live apart from his or her owner or hirer without obtaining a ticket from the owner describing the place and specifying the time duration. Renting directly to slaves, even with permission of owner, is illegal.

1817   No day-hireling slave has the right to demand more compensation than $1.00 for a day's work.

It is unlawful for anyone to sell goods, of a value exceeding $5.00, to a slave without written permission from the slave's owner.

1829   All slaves to be taxed $1.00.

1838   Slaves caught drinking are to be arrested.

1856   Slaves can purchase liquor with a written pass from their master, although slaves can be arrested for drinking in grog-shops or coffee houses in the city.

1857   Any person buying or selling any produce or commodity to a slave must have written consent from the owner or employer of the slave.

Norfolk

1844   Male slaves who are hired out must obtain licenses at $1.00 per slave, and slaves so licensed are entitled to receive $1.00 for every day while employed, or 12½¢ per hour for less than a full day.

1852   Passes are necessary for slaves who are out after 8:30 P.M. in the winter and 9:30 P.M. in the summer.

Richmond

1806   Slaves hired by the year must be registered.

No slave shall sell "eatables" or provisions.

1811   No slave shall sell provisions or vegetables unless granted written permission from his owner or employer.

1837   No slave or free person of color can buy fruits or provisions in the Public Markets for any person other than those to whom they belong or are hired, unless they have written permission.

1838   Tax on all slaves over twelve years old is set at $1.00.

Revises above to $1.25.

1851   Slaves need written permission to sell or buy anything at the market.

1859   Passes are required for slaves out after hours, and written permission is needed for living out by the night.

No slaves are allowed to hire themselves out.

Renting of houses to slaves is illegal.

No slaves shall be paid directly for board. Instead, every owner, hirer, or other employer of a slave in Richmond must provide food and lodging for such slaves upon his own premises or arrange board and lodging for them with some free persons and directly compensate such a person. It is not illegal for a slave who has a wife living in the city to stay with her at the house of her master.

No liquor is to be sold to slaves.

No one can employ a slave without written permission from the slave's owner.

Saint Louis

1835   No slave is to be out after 10:00 P.M. in the summer and 9:00 P.M. in the winter without a written pass from his owner.

Savannah

1839   All Negroes who are hired out or are employed out of their owner's family or house are to take out badges. Price schedule (with 1854 prices shown for comparison):

	1839	1854
Cabinet makers, house or ship carpenters, caulkers, bricklayers, blacksmiths, tailors, barbers, bakers, and butchers	$10.56	$10.00
Coopers, painters, wood sawyers, pilots, fishermen, boatmen, and grass cutters	8.56	8.00
Female porters or laborers	3.06	2.50
Male porters or laborers	4.56	4.00
Venders of small wares and hucksters	8.88	
Venders of vegetables and grist in the market (1840)	8.88	

No badge shall be issued to any slave for the sale of small wares, unless the slave is incapable of doing hard labor.

No slave shall live apart from his owner without first obtaining a ticket.

Slave mechanics can work on contracts, that is self-hire, only if they obtain written permission from their owners.

1854   Slave mechanics cannot self hire unless they receive written permission from their owners.

Slaves and free persons of color cannot vend goods, wares, or liquor unless in the presence of a white person.

A meeting of more than seven slaves or free persons of color constitutes illegal assemblage, except in the presence of a white person or during Sunday worship. The teaching of slaves or free persons of color to read and write is illegal.

Tickets are required for slaves who are out at night.

Revised badge fees, see 1839.

1857   No slave can butcher meat unless in the presence of a white employer.

All slaves who are hired out must take out badges unless they are hired in a white person's family or dwelling, (amends the 1839 ordinance).

Slaves over 12 and under 60 years old are taxed $3.00; those twelve and under, 50¢.

Notes

Chapter 1

1. Although the American experience with slavery involved limited urban growth, this is not true either of the ancient world or of Latin America. See, for example, A. H. M. Jones, "Slavery in the Ancient World," in *Slavery in Classical Antiquity*, ed. Moses Finley (Cambridge, England: Heffer, 1960), for a discussion of Athenian slavery; and see Mary Karasch, "From Porterage to Proprietorship: African Occupations in Rio de Janeiro, 1808–1850," in Stanley L. Engerman and Eugene D. Genovese, eds., *Race and Slavery in the Western Hemisphere: Quantitative Studies* (Princeton: Princeton University Press, 1975), and Herbert Klein, *Slavery in the Americas: A Comparative Study of Virginia and Cuba* (Chicago: University of Chicago Press, 1967), for descriptions of Latin American experiences.

I have assumed that the reader is familiar with some of the recent additions to the economics of slavery literature. Robert W. Fogel and Stanley L. Engerman's book *Time on the Cross* (Boston: Little Brown, 1974), provides an excellent background for those who are unfamiliar with this topic and also presents new data and conclusions. Much of the important work on this subject by other economists and historians has been summarized in this two-volume work. Major precedents to Fogel and Engerman's work are, in particular, A. H. Conrad and J. R. Meyer, "The Economics of Slavery in the Ante-bellum South," *Journal of Political Economy* 66 (April 1958): 95–130, reprinted in *The Economics of Slavery and Other Studies in Econometric History* (Chicago: Aldine Publishing Co., 1964), pp. 43–92; R. Evans, Jr., "The Economics of American Negro Slavery, 1830 to 1860," (Ph.D. diss., University of Chicago, 1959), portions of which are reprinted in *Aspects of Labor Economics*, ed. H. Gregg Lewis (Princeton: Princeton University Press, 1962), pp. 185–243; and Yasukichi Yasuba, "The Profitability and Viability of Plantation Slavery in the United States," *Economic Studies Quarterly* 12 (September 1961): 60–67. Robert S. Starobin, *Industrial Slavery in the Old South* (New York: Oxford University Press, 1970), is an excellent introduction to that topic. It should be noted that industrial and urban slavery in the South were not synonymous, because much industry was an integral part of the agricultural economy and was rural in location, and much urban slave labor had no connection with manufacturing.

2. Frederick Douglass, *My Bondage and My Freedom* (1855; repr. New York: Arno Press and The New York Times, 1968), pp. 147–48.

3. John Elliott Cairnes, *The Slave Power* (1862; repr. New York: Torchbook Edition, 1969), pp. 70–71.

4. Charles H. Wesley, *Negro Labor in the United States, 1850 to 1925* (New York: Vanguard Press, 1927), p. 24.

5. Richard C. Wade, *Slavery in the Cities* (New York: Oxford University Press, 1864), pp. 3, 246.

6. Clement Eaton, "Slave-Hiring in the Upper South: A Step Toward Freedom," *Mississippi Valley Historical Review* 46 (March 1960): 663, 677–78. For a similar view see Richard B. Morris, "The Measure of Bondage in the Slave States," ibid., 41 (1945): 231–39. Charles B. Dew, in "Disciplining Slave Ironworkers in the Ante-bellum South: Coercion, Conciliation, and Accommodation," *American Historical Review* 79 (April 1974): 393–418, takes issue with both Eaton and Morris on this point.

7. See Marion D. de B. Kilson, "Towards Freedom: An Analysis of Slave Revolts in the United States," *Phylon* 25 (2d Quarter 1964): 175–87. Although Kilson reports that 71 percent of "Type I Revolts" involved the urban factor, most of these attempts were in the pre-1820 period.

8. Cairnes, *The Slave Power*, pp. 45–46, 46–47.

9. Ulrich B. Phillips, "The Economic Cost of Slaveholding in the Cotton Belt," *Political Science Quarterly* 20 (June 1905): 259.

10. Lewis Cecil Gray, *History of Agriculture in the Southern United States to 1860*, V. I (Washington: Carnegie Institution, 1933), p. 470.

11. Robert Russel, "The Effects of Slavery upon Southern Economic Progress," *Journal of Southern History* 4 (February 1938): 45.

12. Charles W. Ramsdell, "The Natural Limits of Slavery Expansion," *Mississippi Valley Historical Review* 16, no. 2 (September 1929), 151–71.

13. See Fogel and Engerman, *Time on the Cross*, 2:126–52, for a more complete discussion of economies of scale in the use of slaves.

Chapter 2

1. This finding may be a function of how "urban" is defined. I have used the definition implied by the 1850 and 1860 *Federal Population Censuses*—incorporated towns of over 2,500 persons. I have eliminated some "towns" that were obviously rural. (The number of slaves as a percentage of the population was very high.) Even though I attempted to remove rural areas, some of the newer cities and towns might still include such places, although the omission of many unincorporated towns from the census biases these figures in the opposite direction.

2. In a review of *Time on the Cross*, Herbert Gutman claims that "the 1848 Charleston census . . . is a thoroughly dubious source . . . [because that] census was far from complete and incorrectly counted male slaves and especially male free Blacks and whites." (Gutman, "The World Two Cliometricians Made," *Journal of Negro History* 60 [January 1975]: p. 103.) Gutman claims that 79 percent of the whites, 72 percent of the free blacks, and 27 percent of the slaves are missing from this census count of occupations (p. 104). However, he has failed to observe that Phillips's reporting of the 1848 *Census of Charleston* listed only *manual* occupations (see the notes to table 2). This explains the seemingly large undercount of whites and free blacks who had managerial, proprietary, and clerking

positions. I have no explanation of Gutman's statement that 1,170 white males were listed in this census (p. 104), because the numbers which Phillips reports sum to 1,406. (See also table 11 for the occupational distribution of slaves taken from the same censuses.)

3. Robert E. Gallman, "Trends in the Size Distribution of Wealth in the Nineteenth Century: Some Speculations," in National Bureau of Economic Research, *Six Papers on the Size Distribution of Wealth and Income*, ed. Lee Soltow (New York: Columbia University Press, 1969), pp. 22–23. The wealth distribution of a sample of cotton counties yields that 59 percent of the wealth was held by the top 10 percent of the population and 17 percent by the richest 1 percent. Slaves are treated as wealth but not as potential property holders in both the urban and rural samples.

4. The urban data can be compared to the percentages of foreign born in the free population in 1860: Alabama 2.3, Georgia 2.0, Kentucky 6.4, Louisiana 21.5, Maryland 12.9, Missouri 15.0, South Carolina 3.3, Virginia 3.2 (*source: Federal Population Census*, 1860). The greater percentages for Louisiana, Maryland, and Missouri are almost entirely accounted for by their large cities. New Orleans, for example, contained 43 percent of Louisiana's total free population.

5. Mobile and Savannah are exceptions. Their free Negro populations were never large and did not grow substantially from 1820 to 1860. See table 1.

6. John Blassingame has claimed that "in 1850 the slaves belonging to inhabitants of a city had been credited to that city regardless of where the blacks actually resided in the state. The procedure was reversed in 1860: slaves living in a city were credited to that city regardless of where their masters lived." (Blassingame, "The Afro-Americans: From Mythology to Reality," in William H. Cartwright and R. L. Watson, Jr., eds., *The Reinterpretation of American History and Culture* [Washington, D.C.: National Council for the Social Studies, 1973]). But Blassingame has no evidence for his assertion. In addition, hiring from the city to the country and vice versa appears small enough so that even if the two censuses used different definitions, the resulting figures would not be heavily biased. The extent of hiring from or to the city can be determined from the 1860 returns, which listed slaves with their hirer but also, for some cities, gave their owners' name and location. To the extent that Blassingame's assertion is correct *and* that hiring from the city to the country was more common than the reverse, some of the decline in the urban slave population from 1850 to 1860 (see chapter 4) can be attributed to this factor.

7. Because most of these data on large "usership" come from the 1860 census they refer to actual slave use and not merely to ownership.

8. The labor force is defined here as the population between 15 and 60 years old. In 1860 there were 3,370 males employed in tobacco factories in Henrico County, and 1,310 in Campbell County.

9. Joseph C. Robert, *The Tobacco Kingdom* (Gloucester, Mass.: Peter Smith, 1965), pp. 197–98. He states, "In 1850 58% of the hands employed in the Virginia factories were owned by the manufacturers, while 42% were hired. By 1860 48% were owned, 52% were hired" (p. 198).

10. See chapter 3, especially table 8 for a more detailed description of slave hiring.

Chapter 3

1. Minutes of Council, 1822, Chatham County City Hall, Reel #194092 in Georgia Historical Society, p. 41.

2. Ibid., p. 74.

3. *A Digest of all the Ordinances of the City of Savannah*, C. S. Henry, ed., (Savannah: Purse's Print, 1854), p. 328.

4. Slavery Petitions, South Carolina Department of Archives and History, Columbia, S.C. For further work on white and slave artisans in Charleston see Leonard Stavisky, "The Negro Artisan in the South Atlantic States: 1800–1860" (Ph.D. diss., Columbia University, 1958).

5. See Charles Dew, *Ironmaker to the Confederacy* (New Haven: Yale University Press, 1966) for a detailed description of Anderson's operations.

6. *A Digest of the Ordinances of the City Council of Charleston*, 1844, p. 177; *The Ordinances of the Borough of Norfolk*, 1845, p. 245.

7. Frederick Douglass, *Life and Times of Frederick Douglass* (1892; repr. New York: Collier Books, 1962).

8. Slavery Petitions, South Carolina Department of Archives and History, Columbia, S.C.

9. Minutes of Council, Chatham County City Hall, Reel #194093 in Georgia Historical Society, p. 337.

10. Robert Russell, in *North America: Its Agriculture and Climate* (Edinburgh, 1857), estimated that slaves working in Richmond tobacco factories earned from two to five dollars a month in bonuses (p. 152). Other estimates run even higher. See Robert, *The Tobacco Kingdom*, p. 204.

11. Charleston Court of General Sessions, South Carolina Department of Archives and History, Columbia, S.C.

12. See Robert S. Starobin, ed., *Denmark Vesey: The Slave Conspiracy of 1822* (New Jersey: Prentice Hall, 1970), pt. 2, "Americans React to the Plot." Although many Southerners reiterated their proslavery arguments in reaction to the Vesey insurrection, some expressed doubts about the efficacy of the institution.

13. A petition by Charlestonians in the autumn of 1822 asked among other items for: (1) the removal of all free blacks, (2) limitations on hiring mechanics and the provision that any who were hired should be under the immediate control of their master, and (3) a prohibition against slaves' living out. Although this particular legislation against slaves appears not to have been passed, Greene and Woodson report that after 1822 "each free Negro mechanic of Charleston, who was occupied within the patrol limits of the city, was assessed $10." See Lorenzo J. Greene and Carter G. Woodson, *The Negro Wage Earner* (Washington, D.C.: Association for the Study of Negro Life and History, 1930), p. 16.

14. Douglass, *Life and Times*, p. 185.

15. See Fogel and Engerman, *Time on the Cross*, vol. 1, esp. chap. 4.

16. Hiring and living-out arrangements were also common practices among slaves in fourth- and fifth-century Athens. See A. H. M. Jones, "Slavery in the Ancient World," in Moses Finley, ed., *Slavery in Classical Antiquity*. Herbert Klein, in *Slavery in the Americas: A Comparative Study of Virginia and Cuba* (Chicago: University of Chicago Press, 1967), stated that Havana slaves were also hired out and lived apart from their masters as "the inevitable consequences of skilled urban slavery in Cuba" (p. 190).

17. Guardianship accounts are official registers of the goods and services belonging to a minor which were a part of an estate in probate. Many minors whose relatives died received the hire rates from slaves who belonged to such an estate. The accounts give a description of the slave, the name of the hirer, the net hire rate, and the duration of the hiring period. The majority of those hired for less than a full year were contracted for periods of six or three months.

18. Eaton, in "Slave Hiring in the Upper South," discusses problems in using and interpreting the hiring data in the 1860 census manuscripts.

19. Robert, in *The Tobacco Kingdom*, states that "the basic 5 percent hiring fee fluctuated with the variety of services promised" (p. 201). Clement Eaton cites slave broker Robert Hill's 1841 advertisement in the Richmond *Whig* as stating that his fee was the usual "7½ percent for hiring out, bonding, collecting the same" ("Slave Hiring in the Upper South," p. 665).

20. See Dismal Swamp Land Company receipts 1800–1859 in Duke University Archives.

21. For example, the Midlothian Coal Mining Company advertised in the 30 December 1854 *Richmond Enquirer* that "hands hired by the Midlothian Company can be insured in Richmond . . . ; and as two physicians attend the hospital at the mines, medical attendance for the year can be secured by paying a fee of $3 per hand."

22. *Mobile City Code of Laws*, 1858, p. 42; *A General Digest of the Ordinances and Resolutions of the Corporation of New Orleans, 1831*, p. 139; *The Ordinances of the Borough of Norfolk*, 1845, pp. 244–45; *The Charters and Ordinances of the City of Richmond*, 1859, pp. 200–201.

23. *A Digest of All the Ordinances of the City of Savannah*, 1854, pp. 339–40; *A Digest of the Ordinances of the City Council of Charleston*, 1818, p. 185.

24. The 31 August 1849 *Charleston Courier* reported that funds from badge sales were $13,750 for the year, whereas city taxes of the same year were $131,932. Since there were about fifteen thousand slaves who could be hired out in that year, and badges ranged from two to seven dollars, the badge sales income implies a large hiring percentage and a substantial level of skill.

25. Minutes of Council, 1812, Chatham County City Hall, reel #194091 in Georgia Historical Society, p. 10.

26. William Harris Garland Papers, Southern Historical Collection, University of North Carolina, Chapel Hill, 31 December 1848.

27. *Charters and Ordinances of Richmond*, 1859, p. 196; *Digest and Ordinances of Savannah*, 1854, p. 346; *A Collection of the Ordinances in the*

City of Mobile, 1843, p. 139; *Mobile City Code of Laws*, 1858, p. 173; the 1843 Mobile restrictions required the slaveowner to register the self-hired slave and to obtain a badge for one dollar. The 1858 legislation is rather ambiguous, because it specified that self-hire was illegal but provided for the hiring of slaves "by the day," which could only mean self-hire, since slave users did not usually hire slaves on a daily basis.

28. See Henry W. Farnam, *Chapters in the History of Social Legislation in the U.S. to 1860* (Washington, D.C.: Carnegie Institution of Washington, 1938), pp. 191–92.

29. See John Hebron Moore, "Simon Gray, Riverman: A Slave Who Was Almost Free," *Mississippi Valley Historical Review* 49 (December 1962), 472–84, for a description of the life of one self-hired slave.

30. *Mobile City Code of Laws*, 1858, p. 173; *Ordinances of the City of Charleston*, 1854, p. 52.

31. The number 9.7 was obtained by dividing the number of free blacks (3,237) listed as living in Charleston in the 1860 *Federal Population Census* by the number of houses occupied by free blacks (334). The comparable figure for whites is 10.1. Data on the number of white families living in Charleston in 1861 suggests that, in general, each house was occupied by more than one family. The population data in the *Census of the City of Charleston, 1861* are slightly different from those in the federal census. If the former data are used, one gets 11.3 free blacks per house, which implies that about 13 percent of all slaves lived apart from their owners.

32. The 1857 *Laws and General Ordinances of the City of New Orleans* contains a provision which could be interpreted as rendering living out illegal. It states that no slave can rent a room or house even with permission of his owner but does not seem to rule out the owner's renting it for his slave (pp. 257–58).

33. *Charters and Ordinances of Richmond*, 1859, pp. 196–97.

34. *A Collection of Ordinances in Mobile*, 1843, p. 139.

35. This percentage was computed by summing the male slaves listed in table 11 from apprentices to wharf builders. This yielded a figure of 582 slaves, which was divided by the subtotal, 3,496, giving 17 percent. If there are omitted slaves, this procedure assumes that they were distributed identically to those whose occupations were given. Since it is possible (as suggested in chap. 2) that many slaves who were used primarily as domestics had some other skills as well, 17 percent can be viewed as a lower bound.

36. The 1850 probate records gave appraisals for 340 slaves, of whom 8 had listed skills. The 1860 records show 475 slave appraisals with 62 skilled. One estate in 1860 was of a Mr. Tom Lucas, who had a highly skilled group of slaves. One can eliminate the possible bias of including this particular estate by subtracting Lucas's slaves from the totals. This yields 209 slaves with 23 skilled for 1860. Although I am aware of the limitations of these data, they do indicate an increase over time of skills for urban slaves.

37. Slavery Petitions, South Carolina Department of Archives and History, Columbia, S.C.

38. See Fogel and Engerman, *Time on the Cross*.

39. Slavery Petitions, South Carolina Department of Archives and History, Columbia, South Carolina.

40. Specific skills are those which are valued by a small number of owners, possibly even one. They include knowledge of a particular household or business, and training which can be used in a particular enterprise. These are distinguished from general skills which can be utilized in any household or business. The ability to read and write is considered to be one of the most general skills. For a more detailed discussion of specific and general training, and human capital theory see G. Becker, *Human Capital* (New York: National Bureau of Economic Research, 1964).

41. Laws in most Southern states included a provision for the sale and deportation of any slave found guilty of manslaughter, or for the death of such a slave with compensation awarded the owner. This was to prevent slaveowners from protecting their slaves in murder cases or from hiding evidence to save their investment.

Chapter 4

1. Average annual rates were computed by use of the formula:
$$x_{t+10} = x_t \, e^{r(10)},$$
which is solved for r.

2. When reporting these numbers in average annual rate-of-change form, I am assuming that population growth was fairly steady between the census years. In using the data for the model in chapter 5, I make a weaker assumption. One can more realistically assume that even if the population data were not smooth, the explanation for the observed data given by the model would also be applicable to nonobserved changes. That is, the parameters of the model are assumed to be constant.

Some cities performed their own censuses during years other than federal census dates. The results below indicate that there were no violent population changes with the decades given for Charleston and Richmond.

Charleston	1820	1824	1830	1840	1848	1850
Slave population	12,652	13,852	15,354	14,673	17,655	19,532
	1820–24	*1824–30*	*1820–30*	*1840–48*	*1848–50*	*1840–50*
Average annual rate of change in slave population	+.023	+.017	+.019	+.023	+.051	+.029

Richmond	1850	1854	1860
Slave population	9,927	10,884	11,699
	1850–54	*1854–60*	*1850–60*
Average annual rate of change in slave population	+.026	+.012	+.016

Sources: *Charleston Courier*, 7 August 1824; *Census of Charleston*, 1848; *Richmond Enquirer*, 26 October 1854.

3. Census figures show that black fertility declined substantially after 1880. See U.S. Bureau of the Census, *Negro Population, 1790–1915* (Washington, D.C.: G.P.O., 1918), p. 290. Black fertility is given at 760 children 0 to 4 years of age per thousand women 15 to 44 in 1880, but only at 519 in 1910. The 1910 figure is reduced to 248 if only cities of more than 25,000 persons are considered. The same statistic is 609 for Southern areas not including these cities. These figures further accentuate how low some of the slave fertility numbers, in table 18, part B, are. Robert Higgs, *Competition and Coercion: Blacks in the American Economy, 1865–1915*, pp. 21–23 (forthcoming), accounts for this decline in fertility by the reduced mortality and increased income opportunities in cities.

4. The age at which slaves earned their maintenance, the break-even point, was about ten, with females earning nonnegative hires about a year before males. See Fogel and Engerman, *Time on the Cross*, vol. 1, chapter 3.

5. Richard Sutch finds very similar results in a fertility study of the New and Old South. He concludes that there were more slave children in the Old South per slave female, and that this could be due to selective migration. That is, less fertile and "unmarried" female slaves were sold to the New South region, where the growing season was longer and where pregnancies would be more costly. See Richard Sutch, "Breeding Slaves for Sale and Westward Expansion of Slavery, 1850–1860," in Engerman and Genovese, eds., *Race and Slavery in the Western Hemisphere*.

6. See Conrad and Meyer, "The Economics of Slavery in the Ante-Bellum South," p. 69n. Also see Fogel and Engerman, *Time on the Cross*, vol. 1, chapter 1.

7. W. E. B. DuBois, *The Suppression of the African Slave Trade to the United States, 1638 to 1870* (New York: Longmans, Green and Co., 1896), pp. 90–91.

8. A survivor rate of 0.80 seems more reasonable for 1800–1810 than one of 0.82 or 0.83 characteristic of the 1830–40 period. Survivor rates give the percentage of the population now living which is expected to be surviving ten years hence. The computation given above also assumes that 30 percent of the population in 1810 was under ten years of age. See Fogel and Engerman, *Time on the Cross*, 2:43–48, for a description of the exact method which I have used.

9. See W. D. Postell, *The Health of Slaves on Southern Plantations* (Baton Rouge: Louisiana State University Press, 1951). These epidemics can explain some fraction of the decline in the slave populations in cities during the two decades, 1830 to 1840 and 1850 to 1860. Cities such as New Orleans normally had severe epidemics when rural areas experienced moderate health problems. But this is neither a sufficient nor a complete explanation for the violent changes in slave populations which the cities underwent.

10. Ulrich B. Phillips, *American Negro Slavery in the United States* (Baton Rouge: Louisiana State University Press, 1966), p. 370.

11. Robert Evans, Jr., "The Economics of Negro Slavery, 1830 to 1860."

12. The percent difference in the prices between slaves who were appraised and then sold is smaller than between aggregate numbers on sales and appraisals. That is, the average appraised price of specific slaves who were later sold is closer to their actual sale price than the average data on appraisals and sales indicate. This might mean that the group of slaves in the appraised data were somehow different from those in the sales data. One possible difference is that sales may have been more highly concentrated in the prime ages than were appraisals. This finding can also be the result of a more honest appraisal when the appraisers knew a slave would be sold from the estate. Further work on this problem is being done by Fogel and Engerman.

13. See Fogel and Engerman, *Time on the Cross*, vol. 1, chapter 2. They estimate that 84 percent of female slaves over the age of fourteen sold in New Orleans were unmarried. This and related information suggest that slaves who were sold to the New South were not part of family groups. They were, instead, single, widowed, or divorced.

14. See Bureau of the Census, *Historical Statistics*, p. 120 and 122.

Chapter 5

1. Note that the elasticity in (4) is ϵ_i not e_i, because the price term in this equation includes T_i. Equation (5) shows that the relationship between the two elasticities is: $e_i = [\epsilon_i/(1 + \phi)]$. The value ϵ_i is the elasticity of quantity with respect to the net hire rate (or price) plus yearly taxation, and so on (or present value of taxation), and e_i is the elasticity of quantity with respect to only the net hire or price.

T_i could have been added to P_i in equation (1), but I did not do this for two reasons. The first is that data on P_i are available, but there is no complete series on T_i (see chapter 3). Second, the historical literature which stresses changes in T_i separates these forces from those on price, as I have done in equation (5).

2. An assumption implicit in this analysis is that the larger rural market determines P_i, and therefore the level of costs specific to the city, T_i, does not become incorporated into P_i.

3. License fees or badges for hiring out slaves were, in some cities, a graduated tax, being a function of the hiring rate itself. See chapter 4 on badge fees in Charleston and Savannah. For these cities this portion of T appears to have been less than one-twentieth of the hire rate. Other components of T are more difficult to compute.

4. This is simply the condition that all demand functions be downward sloping.

5. I would like to thank H. Gregg Lewis for suggesting this method of analyzing equation (3).

6. If slaves on the one hand, and free whites and blacks on the other, are substitutes, then the wage of free workers, P_f, would be positively corre-

lated with the price or hire rate for slaves, P. This can be demonstrated by letting $P_f = \lambda P$, where $\lambda > 0$. The demand function, which is assumed in the analysis above, is of the form $Q = D\,P^{-e}$. A more properly specified demand function would include a term for the price of free labor, and could be of the general form, $Q = D'P_f{}^{e_f}\,P^{-e}$, where e_f is the cross elasticity of demand for slave labor with respect to changes in the price of free labor, and is assumed to be a positive number. Substituting from above yields, $Q = \lambda^{e_f} D'P^{-e+e_f}$. Therefore, because P_f is omitted from the regressions, the estimated elasticity of demand for slave labor is actually the sum of the own and the cross elasticities. That is, the own elasticity is underestimated by the magnitude of the cross elasticity. The shift parameter is also biased.

7. Assume that the supply function for slaves can be written as $Q = SP^\gamma$, where γ is the elasticity of supply for slaves. This analysis assumed that $\gamma = 0$, or was very small for ten year periods. This can be rationalized in a variety of ways. In the first place, the closing of the international slave trade made the short run supply schedule of labor highly inelastic for even if planters attempted to alter the slave birth rate such efforts would have had no effect on the labor force supply for at least a decade. In addition, contemporary estimates of the number of slaves engaged in production were approximately equal to the number who were physically available in the total population. (See Conrad and Meyer, *The Economics of Slavery*, p. 76). Furthermore, the changes in the rate at which the slave population grew, from 1820 to 1860, seem to have been affected mainly by the importation of adult females during the period prior to 1807, the cholera and yellow fever epidemics of the 1830s and 1850s, and changes in the fertility rates, which appear to have been independent of demand considerations. (See M. Zelnick, "Fertility of the American Negro in 1830 to 1850," *Population Studies* 20 (July 1966): 77–83.)

8. Rural Virginia and Louisiana deflated prices were used for the weighted average price. The shares calculated as weights are:

	1820	1830	1840	1850	1860
Lower South	.10	.25	.28	.34	.40
Upper South	.90	.75	.72	.66	.60

Lower South is defined to include Alabama, Arkansas, Louisiana, Mississippi, Missouri, and Texas. Upper South includes all other slaveholding states.

9. The following tabulation of the "t" distribution for 1 and 2 degrees of freedom for various levels of significance is helpful in interpreting the coefficients and constant terms. Because of the very limited number of observations, the usual 5 percent level of significance cannot be used. In addition, even where the coefficients are rather insignificant, they are still the maximum likelihood estimates. Furthermore, the homogeneity of the results reniforces the use of coefficients which otherwise would be rejected at even the 20 percent level.

The "t" Distribution for 1 and 2 Degrees of Freedom
(Probability: 2 Tailed)

Degrees of Freedom	.5	.4	.3	.2	.1	.05	.02	.01
1	1.000	1.376	1.963	3.078	6.314	12.706	31.821	63.657
2	.816	1.061	1.386	1.886	2.920	4.303	6.965	9.925

Source: R. A. Fisher and F. Yates, *Statistical Tables* (London: Diver and Boyd, 1938), p. 26.

10. Claudia Goldin, "The Economics of Urban Slavery, 1820 to 1860" (Ph.D. diss., University of Chicago, 1972); parts reprinted in "A Model to Explain the Relative Decline of Urban Slavery," in E. Genovese and S. Engerman, eds., *Race and Slavery in the Western Hemisphere* (Princeton: Princeton University Press, 1975).

11. It should be noted that the urban aggregate results in table 27 are not for a pooled regression but for a single urban area. Each of the three equations has four observations. The slave population and the labor force data underlying these results are the summed data for each of the constituent cities expressed in growth rate form. I did run pooled regressions for each of the three urban aggregates, and the results are given below. These results are quite similar to the nonpooled aggregated regression coefficients but have more observations and, therefore, larger degrees of freedom.

	$\hat{D}*$	$-\hat{e}$	R^2	$\hat{D}*$	$\hat{b}$	$-\hat{e}$	R^2	n
Old South	.031	−.607	.365	.019	.380	−.533	.435	16
	(4.34)[a]	(−2.84)[a]		(1.70)[c]	(1.26)	(−2.45)[a]		
New South	.034	.103	.006	−.014	1.011	−.588	.804	8
	(1.57)	(.19)		(−.92)	(4.51)[a]	(−1.94)[c]		
Border States	.041	−1.33	.399	.007	.443	−.980	.509	16
	(2.87)[a]	(−3.50)[a]		(.30)	(1.70)[c]	(−2.15)[b]		

[a]Shows significance at the 5% level.
[b]Shows significance at the 10% level.
[c]Shows significance at the 20% level.

The number of observations for both the Border States and Old South city regressions is 16 and that for the New South is 8. The urban slave labor force was used for $Q*$. Deflated Virginia City prices were used for the Border State and Old South cities, and deflated Louisiana slave labor force prices were used for the New South cities. (See footnote 28 for a discussion of the equality of these coefficients with those from the unpooled, disaggregated regressions.)

12. See E. Vickrey, "The Economics of the Negro Migration, 1900–1960" (Ph.D. diss., University of Chicago, 1969).

13. Equation (11′) is slightly different from equation (11) because the price term is for urban slaves. The theoretical framework does not allow

for heterogeneous labor inputs, but the empirical work accounts for them by using different prices.

14. The weights used are: Old South, .52; New South, .30; and Border State Cities, .18.

15. The pooled cross section-time series results, given in note 11, yield a not much different equation: $Q^*_c = .038 - .63P^*_c$.

16. This differs from equation (12) because the price term is for rural slaves, P^*_r. This is the same distinction made between equations (11) and (11′).

17. The coefficient on C^*, $\hat{b}$, was multiplied by the mean of C^*, and this was then added to $\hat{D}'^*$ to get $\hat{D}^*$.

18. The urban and rural equations under this assumption would have been: $Q^*_c = .036 - eP^*$, and $Q^*_r = .025 - eP^*$. The intercepts have been taken from equations (15) and (16).

19. This was computed using the assumption that both rural and urban demand schedules had an elasticity of demand equal to that of the total, that is $e_t = e_r = e_c = e = .08$, and were of the form given in note 18.

20. The size of e_r was also affected by the size of the elasticity of demand for cotton. The elasticity of demand for raw cotton has been computed in one study as between .31 and .65. See G. Wright, "An Econometric Study of Cotton Production and Trade, 1830 to 1860," *Review of Economics and Statistics* 53 (May 1971): 111–19.

21. For a discussion of these scale economies, see Fogel and Engerman, *Time on the Cross*, especially 2:126–52, and Jacob Metzer, "Efficient Operation and Economies of Scale in the Ante-Bellum Southern Plantation" (The Hebrew University of Jerusalem, September 1974, mimeographed).

22. See table 3 for urban data on the percentage foreign-born. The cities contained almost the entire foreign-born section of each state. For example, 21 percent of all Louisiana free persons were foreign-born, but subtracting Orleans Parish reduces this to 6.5 percent. This same datum for Virginia is reduced from 3.2 to 2.7 percent when Henrico County is omitted.

23. See Fogel and Engerman, *The Reinterpretation of American Economic History*, pp. 330–31.

24. Although this market-size proxy serves to diminish $\hat{D}^*$ in some cases, it increases it in others. The reasons for this have been discussed previously and involve the use of Q^*_{fp} in the substitute labor market wage equation.

25. H. A. Trexler, *Slavery in Missouri, 1804 to 1865* (Baltimore: Johns Hopkins Press, 1914), p. 185.

26. Ibid.

27. The values of e in the sensitivity analysis for the cities are greater than those for all slave states, because the maximum likelihood estimates for the total were much lower than those for the cities.

28. The aggregated results presented in table 27 are not for a pooled cross-section and time series. They are, instead, for an aggregated group of cities, where each observation is the growth rate for the sum of each city's slave population, labor force, and so on. Pooled regional regressions were performed, and their results are given in note 11. The interpretation of these results is different from that of the aggregated data. These pooled

regressions, however, can be compared to the nonpooled, disaggregated ones to see whether regional definitions are sensible. One can use a test of the equality of coefficients (an "F" or a Chow test) to determine whether constraining the coefficients in the pooled aggregate is an accurate procedure. This hypothesis cannot be rejected for any of the three pooled regressions, because the sum of squared residuals in the constrained equations is not very large in comparison to that for the unconstrained ones. That is, the constrained or pooled regressions appear to obey the same relation as the unconstrained ones, and therefore the regional distinctions are meaningful. To perform this test, the Charleston, Savannah, and Saint Louis data had to be rerun using the Virginia City prices, and the test was done for the labor force regressions containing the Q^*_{fp} variable.

29. There are obvious interconnections among the economic, social, and political factors which this simple model has not incorporated. Most important among these, immigration to a city may have been affected by the social climate, and political factors concerning the security of slavery in Border areas may have motivated some of the sales from this region.

30. These results differ from those used elsewhere in this book, because they are taken from table 27, part A. They do not account for any components of D^*.

Chapter 6

1. See table 27, part C. Louisville and New Orleans have $\hat{D}'^* < 0$, implying that the omitted variables had a negative impact on D^*.

2. There is only indirect evidence on this point. The cities which had the smallest $\hat{D}'^*$, in general, had the largest immigration percentages.

3. See Fogel and Engerman, *Time on the Cross*, vol. 1, especially chapter 6, and Metzer, "Efficient Operation and Economies of Scale in the Ante-Bellum Southern Plantation."

4. Gavin Wright estimates that the rate of demand growth for cotton was 2.58% on an average annual basis in the 1830s, 4.81% in the 1840s, and 4.50% in the 1850s. But the postbellum period showed a drastic slowing down in this figure. The 1870s figure is 1.34% and that for the 1880s is 1.38%. See G. Wright, "Cotton Competition and the Post-Bellum Recovery of the American South," *Journal of Economic History* 34 (September 1974), 610–35.

Epilogue

1. The 1890 *Federal Census* is the earliest recording of occupation by race in a printed census.

2. Much has been written on this general topic. Charles Wesley, in *Negro Labor in the United States*, chaps. 6–8, has a good discussion on black skills, the effects of unions, and the demands of modern industrialization. W. E. B. DuBois and Augustus G. Dill's "The Negro American Artisan," in *The Negro American* (1912; New York: Arno Press and The New York Times, 1968) contains the results of a questionnaire about the conditions of

the late nineteenth-century black artisan, the effects of unionization, differences in wage rates between black and white artisans, and so on. There is also a discussion of vocational schools, like Tuskegee, founded to train blacks in modern industrial skills. Greene and Woodson, in *The Negro Wage Earner*, also discuss the forces in the late nineteenth century which led to the decline of the black artisan. Higgs, in *Competition and Coercion*, summarizes much of this literature.

3. Although listed occupations differ somewhat among the cities, five cities —Charleston, New Orleans, New York, Philadelphia, and Richmond—all had very similar skilled trades reported. These included apprentices, bakers, blacksmiths, boot and shoemakers, butchers, cabinet makers, carpenters, coopers, machinists, marble cutters, masons, painters, plasterers, plumbers, printers, tailors, upholsterers, and woodworkers.

4. See Gary Becker, *The Economics of Discrimination* (Chicago: University of Chicago Press, 1971), especially chap. 5. This alternative explanation has some further support in the 1890 census data. Two percent of the black labor force in Charleston were professionals (i.e., doctors, lawyers, government officials, clergymen, professors, and teachers), and 6 percent of the whites were. But in New York, 3 percent of the whites and only 0.7 percent of the blacks were in professional occupations. Therefore it is possible that a large and dense enough black community existed in Charleston so that blacks could buy from "their own." Blacks could have been too separated geographically in New York to have the same proportional impact. These data may also be accounted for by income differentials in the two cities and a host of other unexplored factors.

5. *The Census of Charleston for 1848* lists 117 white carpenters, 110 slave, and 27 free black, all in the building trade. This implies that 43.3% of these skilled workers were slaves. See tables 2 and 11.

6. In New York, 0.3 percent of the blacks were carpenters, but only 2 percent of the male labor force was black. Since 56 percent of Charleston's male labor force was black, the New York number was multiplied by 28.

7. Frederick Douglass, paraphrased by Charles Wesley in *Negro Labor in the United States*, pp. 212–13.

8. Greene and Woodson, *The Negro Wage Earner*, p. 168.

9. DuBois and Dill, "The Negro American Artisan," p. 38.

10. See Richard Freeman, "Black and White Economic Differences: Why Did They Last So Long: The Role of Educational Discrimination" (mimeographed, April 1972), for a discussion of the role of government in enforcing discriminatory attitudes. Freeman finds that although Southern blacks increased their education from 1865 to about 1905, at some time in the very early twentieth century expenditures on black relative to white education fell dramatically.

11. Wesley, *Negro Labor in the United States*, p. 186.

Bibliography

Primary Sources

Government Documents

Bureau of the Census. *Historical Statistics of the United States: Colonial Times to 1957*. Washington: U.S. Government Printing Office, 1960.

————. *Negro Population, 1790–1915*. Washington: U.S. Government Printing Office, 1918.

City Directories of the United States, 1820–1860. New Haven: Research Publications, Inc., 1970. (Microfiche.)

U.S. Census Office. *Fourth Census, 1820*. Washington, Gales and Seaton, 1821.

————. *Fifth Census, 1830*. Washington: D. Green, 1832.

————. *Sixth Census, 1840*. Washington: Blair and Rives, 1841.

————. *Seventh Census, 1850*. Washington: Gideon and Company, 1852.

————. *Eighth Census, 1860*. Washington: U.S. Government Printing Office, 1864.

————. *Seventh Census, 1850*. Population Schedules: Alabama, Georgia, Kentucky, Louisiana, Maryland, Mississippi, South Carolina, Virginia, Washington, D.C. Washington: U.S. National Archives, 1850. (Microfilm.)

————. *Eighth Census, 1860*. Population Schedules: Alabama, Georgia, Kentucky, Louisiana, Maryland, Mississippi, South Carolina, Washington, D.C. Washington: U.S. National Archives, 1955. (Microfilm.)

————. *Tenth Census, 1880*. Vol. 28: *Report on the Social Statistics of the Cities*; part 3: *The Southern and Western States*. Washington: U.S. Government Printing Office, 1887.

————. *Eleventh Census, 1890*. Part 2. Washington: U.S. Government Printing Office, 1897.

————. *Mortality, 1850–1860*. South Carolina: Department of Archives and History (Microfilm.)

Note: All U.S. Census Office publications are referred to in the text and notes as *Federal Population Census*, followed by the date of the census.

Newspapers

Charleston Courier (Charleston, South Carolina). 1824–54.
Charleston Mercury (Charleston, South Carolina). 1835.
Louisville Daily Democrat (Louisville, Kentucky). 1858.
Louisville Public Advertiser (Louisville, Kentucky). 1820–27.
New Orleans Bee (New Orleans, Louisiana). 1835–55.
New Orleans Times Picayune (New Orleans, Louisiana). 1830–61.
Richmond Dispatch (Richmond, Virginia). 1852–60.
Richmond Enquirer (Richmond, Virginia). 1831–54.

Archival Material

ALABAMA   Alabama Department of Archives and History, Montgomery

A Collection of the Ordinances . . . In the City of Mobile . . . Mobile, 1835.

A Collection of the Ordinances . . . In the City of Mobile . . . Mobile, 1843.

City of Mobile
Mobile City Code of Laws. Mobile, 1858.

GEORGIA   Georgia Historical Society, Savannah
Ordinances:

A Digest of all the Ordinances of the City of Savannah . . . Ed. Charles S. Henry. Savannah: Purse's Print, 1854.

Code of Savannah, 1858, A Digest of All the Ordinances of the City of Savannah. Ed. Edward G. Wilson. Savannah: John M. Cooper and Co., 1858.

Other Items:
Census of Savannah. Ed. Joseph Bancroft. Savannah, 1848.

Chatham County City Hall. Minutes of Council. 1812–1863.

Mayor's Docket. 1858–1859.

LOUISIANA   New Orleans Public Library, New Orleans
A General Digest of the Ordinances and Resolutions of the Corporation of New Orleans, 1831.

Digest of the Ordinances and Resolutions of the Second Municipality of New Orleans in Force, May 1, 1840.

City of New Orleans City Council Ordinances and Resolutions, January 1848.

The Laws and General Ordinances of the City of New Orleans, 1857.

MISSOURI   City of Saint Louis

Ordinances of the City of St. Louis, 1835.

Ordinances of the City of St. Louis, 1843.

Ordinances of the City of St. Louis, 1845 to 1850.

NORTH CAROLINA   Duke University Library, Durham

Clark, Henry Toole. Financial Papers, 1783–1839.
Dismal Swamp Land Company. Receipts, 1800–1859.
Dunn, John D. Steamboat Payroll Book, 1855–59.
Grist, James R. Papers, 1835–52.
Leslie, Robert. Papers.
Smith, Joseph Belknap. Ledger, 1860–72.

Southern Historical Collection, University of North Carolina Library, Chapel Hill

Battle Family Papers.
Carter, Farish. Papers.
Garland, William Harris. Papers.
Hawkins Family. Papers and Account Books.
Haywood, Earnest. Papers.
Hoke, William Alexander. High Shoal Gold Mining Company Papers.
Louisa Furnace. Account Books and Letter Book, 1835–59.
Mills, Charles. Account Books and Letter Book, 1835–59.
Sparkman Family Papers.
Steele, John. Papers.

SOUTH CAROLINA   South Carolina Department of Archives and History, Columbia

Slavery Petitions

South Caroliniana Library, Columbia

Ordinances:

Charleston Ordinances of the City Council of Charleston from 1783 to 1818. Charleston, 1818.

A Digest of the Ordinances of the City Council of Charleston for the Year 1783 to Oct. 1844. Ed. George B. Eckhard. Charleston: Walker and Burke, 1844.

Ordinances of the City of Charleston from the 19th of August, 1844 to the 14th of September, 1854. Ed. H. Pinckney Walker. Charleston: A. Miller, 1854.

Ordinances of the City of Charleston from 14th of September, 1854 to the 1st of December, 1859. Ed. John R. Horsey. Charleston: Steam Power Press of Walker, Evans and Co., 1859.

Other Items:

Census of the City of Charleston, S.C., for the Year 1861 . . . Ed. Frederick A. Ford. Charleston: Steam Power Presses of Evans and Cogswell, 1861.

Census of the City of Charleston for 1848. Ed. J. P. Dawson and H. W. DeSaussure. Charleston, 1849.

UTAH   Genealogical Society, Salt Lake City

Probate Records, Inventories, Sales, Appraisements, Wills.

Cities: Charleston, South Carolina; Fredericksburg, Virginia; New Orleans, Louisiana; Petersburg, Virginia; Richmond, Virginia; Savannah, Georgia.

Rural: Georgia, Louisiana, Maryland, North Carolina, South Carolina, Tennessee, Virginia.

Bills of Sale of Negro Slaves in the Charleston District of South Carolina, 1799–1861.

VIRGINIA   Virginia Department of Archives and History, Richmond

The Ordinances of the Borough of Norfolk . . . Norfolk, 1845.

The Revised Ordinances of the City of Norfolk . . . Norfolk, 1852.

Richmond Ordinances, March 19, 1804 to May 2, 1821. Unpublished document. Richmond City Hall, Clerk's Office.

Acts of Assembly Relating to the City of Richmond and Ordinances of the Common Council Subsequent to Jan., 1831. Richmond, 1839.

Ordinances Passed by the Council of the City of Richmond since the Year 1839. Richmond, 1847.

157   *Bibliography*

Ordinances of the City of Richmond and Passed by the Council betwwen May, 1851 and January 1852. Richmond, 1852.

The Charters and Ordinances of the City of Richmond with the Declaration of Rights and Constitution of Virginia. Richmond, 1859.

Secondary Sources

Bancroft, Frederic. *Slave Trading in the South.* New York: Frederick Ungar, 1959.
Becker, Gary. *The Economics of Discrimination.* Chicago: University of Chicago Press, 1971.
————. *Human Capital.* New York: National Bureau of Economic Research, 1964.
Blassingame, John. "The Afro-Americans: From Mythology to Reality." In *The Reinterpretation of American History and Culture,* ed. William H. Cartwright and R. L. Watson, Jr. Washington, D.C.: National Council for Social Studies, 1973.
Bruchey, Stuart, ed. *Cotton and the Growth of the American Economy: Sources and Readings.* New York: Harcourt, Brace, and World, 1967.
Cairnes, John Elliott. *The Slave Power.* 1862. New York: Harper (Torchbook Edition), 1969.
Conrad, Alfred H., and Meyer, John R. *The Economics of Slavery and Other Studies in Econometric History.* Chicago: Aldine Publishing Co., 1964.
————. "The Economics of Slavery in the Ante-bellum South." *Journal of Political Economy* 66 (April 1958): 95–130.
Dew, Charles B. "Disciplining Slave Ironworkers in the Antebellum South: Coercion, Conciliation, and Accommodation." *American Historical Review* 79 (April 1974): 393–418.
————. *Ironmaker to the Confederacy.* New Haven: Yale University Press, 1966.
Douglass, Frederick. *Life and Times of Frederick Douglass.* 1892. New York: Collier Books, 1962.
————. *My Bondage and My Freedom.* 1855. New York: Arno Press and The New York Times, 1968.
DuBois, W. E. B. *The Suppression of the African Slave Trade to the United States, 1638 to 1870.* New York: Longmans, Green and Co., 1896.
DuBois, W. E. B., and Dill, Augustus, G. "The Negro American Artisan." 1912. In *The Negro American.* New York: Arno Press and The New York Times, 1968.

Eaton, Clement. "Slave-Hiring in the Upper South: A Step toward Freedom." *Mississippi Valley Historical Review* 46, no. 4 (March 1960): 663–78.

Engerman, Stanley L., and Genovese, Eugene D., eds. *Race and Slavery in the Western Hemisphere: Quantitative Studies.* Princeton: Princeton University Press, 1975.

Evans, Robert, Jr. "The Economics of Negro Slavery, 1830 to 1860." Ph.D. diss., University of Chicago, 1959. Portions reprinted in *Aspects of Labor Economics,* ed. H. Gregg Lewis, pp. 185–243. Princeton: Princeton University Press, 1962.

Farley, Reynolds. "The Urbanization of Negroes in the United States." *Journal of Social History* 1 (Spring 1968): 241–58.

Farnam, Henry W. *Chapters in the History of Social Legislation in the United States to 1860.* Washington, D.C.: Carnegie Institution of Washington, 1938.

Fisher, R. A., and Yates, F. *Statistical Tables for Biological, Agricultural and Medical Research.* London: Diver and Boyd, 1938.

Fogel, Robert W., and Engerman, Stanley L., eds. *The Reinterpretation of American Economic History.* New York: Harper and Row, 1971.

———. *Time on the Cross.* Vol. 1: *The Economics of American Negro Slavery.* Vol. 2: *Evidence and Methods.* Boston: Little Brown, 1974.

Freeman, Richard. "Black and White Economic Differences: Why Did They Last So Long?: The Role of Educational Discrimination." Paper presented at the Cliometrics Conference, Madison, Wisconsin, 27–9 April 1972.

Gallman, Robert E. "Trends in the Size Distribution of Wealth in the Nineteenth Century: Some Speculations." In *Six Papers on the Size Distribution of Wealth and Income,* ed. Lee Soltow. New York: Columbia University Press, 1969.

Genovese, Eugene D. *The Political Economy of Slavery.* New York: Random House (Vintage Books), 1967.

Goldin, Claudia. "The Economics of Urban Slavery, 1820–1860." Ph.D. diss., University of Chicago, 1972. Portions reprinted in "A Model to Explain the Relative Decline of Urban Slavery," in *Race and Slavery in the Western Hemisphere: Quantitative Studies,* ed. E. Genovese and S. Engerman. Princeton: Princeton University Press, 1975.

Gray, Lewis Cecil. *History of Agriculture in the Southern United States to 1860.* Vol. 1. Washington: Carnegie Institution of Washington, 1958.

Greene, Lorenzo J., and Woodson, Carter G. *The Negro Wage Earner.* Washington, D.C.: Association for the Study of Negro Life and History, 1930.

Gutman, Herbert. "The World Two Cliometricians Made." *Journal of Negro History* 60 (January 1975): 53–228.

Higgs, Robert. "Competition and Coercion: Blacks in the American Economy, 1865–1914." University of Washington, 7 June 1974. Mimeographed.

Johnson, D. Gale. "The Allocation of Agricultural Income." *Journal of Farm Economics* 30 (November 1948): 724–47.

Jones, A. H. M. "Slavery in the Ancient World." In *Slavery in Classical Antiquity,* ed. Moses Finley. Cambridge, England: Heffer, 1960.

Karasch, Mary. "From Porterage to Proprietorship: African Occupations in Rio de Janeiro, 1808–1850." In *Race and Slavery in the Western Hemisphere: Quantitative Studies,* ed. E. Genovese and S. Engerman. Princeton: Princeton University Press, 1975.

Kilson, Marion D. de B. "Towards Freedom: An Analysis of Slave Revolts in the United States." *Phylon* 25 (Second Quarter 1964): 175–87.

Klein, Herbert. *Slavery in the Americas: A Comparative Study of Virginia and Cuba.* Chicago: University of Chicago Press, 1967.

Lebergott, Stanley. *Manpower in Economic Growth: The United States Record Since 1800.* New York: McGraw-Hill, 1964.

Metzer, Jacob. "Efficient Operation and Economies of Scale in the Ante-Bellum Southern Plantation." The Hebrew University of Jerusalem, September 1974. Mimeographed.

Moore, John H. "Simon Gray, Riverman: A Slave Who Was Almost Free." *Mississippi Valley Historical Review* 49 (December 1962): 472–84.

Morris, Richard B. "The Measure of Bondage in the Slave States." *Mississippi Valley Historical Review* 41 (1954): 231–39.

National Bureau of Economic Research. *Aspects of Labor Economics.* Edited by H. Gregg Lewis. Princeton: Princeton University Press, 1962.

———. *Trends in the American Economy in the Nineteenth Century.* Conference on Research in Income and Wealth, vol. 24. Princeton: Princeton University Press. 1966.

Phillips, Ulrich B. *American Negro Slavery in the United States.* Baton Rouge: Louisiana State University Press, 1966.

———. "The Economic Cost of Slaveholding in the Cotton Belt." *Political Science Quarterly* 20 (June 1905): 257–75.

————. *The Slave Economy of the Old South*. Baton Rouge: Louisiana State University Press, 1968.

Postell, William Dosite. *The Health of Slaves on Southern Plantations*. Baton Rouge: Louisiana State University Press, 1951.

Ramsdell, Charles W. "The Natural Limits of Slavery Expansion." *Mississippi Valley Historical Review* 16, no. 2 (September 1929): 151–71.

Reinders, Robert C. *End of An Era: New Orleans, 1850 to 1860*. New Orleans: Pelican Publishing Co., 1964.

Robert, Joseph C. *The Tobacco Kingdom*. Gloucester, Mass.: Peter Smith, 1965.

Russel, Robert R. "The General Effects of Slavery upon Southern Economic Progress." *Journal of Southern History* 4 (February 1938): 34–54.

Russell, Robert. *North America: Its Agriculture and Climate*. Edinburgh, 1857.

Starobin, Robert S. *Denmark Vesey: The Slave Conspiracy of 1822*. Englewood Cliffs, N.J.: Prentice-Hall, 1970.

————. *Industrial Slavery in the Old South*. New York: Oxford University Press, 1970.

Stavisky, Leonard. "The Negro Artisan in the South Atlantic States: 1800–1860." Ph.D. diss., Columbia University, 1958.

Trexler, Harrison Anthony. *Slavery in Missouri, 1804 to 1865*. Baltimore: The Johns Hopkins University Press, 1914.

Vickrey, Ed. "The Economics of the Negro Migration, 1900–1960." Ph.D. diss., University of Chicago, 1969.

Wade, Richard D. *Slavery in the Cities*. New York: Oxford University Press, 1964.

Wesley, Charles H. *Negro Labor in the United States, 1850 to 1925*. New York: Vanguard Press, 1927.

Wright, Gavin. "An Econometric Study of Cotton Production and Trade, 1830 to 1860." *Review of Economics and Statistics* 53 (May 1971): 111–19.

————. "Cotton Competition and the Post-Bellum Recovery of the American South." *Journal of Economic History* 34 (September 1974): 610–35.

Yasuba, Yasukichi. "The Profitability and Viability of Plantation Slavery in the United States." *The Economic Studies Quarterly* 12 (September 1961): 60–67.

Zelnick, M. "Fertility of the American Negro in 1830 and 1850." *Population Studies* 20 (July 1966): 77–83.

Index

This index primarily references material in the text and does not attempt a complete indexing of the tables. Readers desiring data on population, fertility, labor force, occupations, demand elasticities, demand shift parameters, and so on should consult the List of Tables at the front of this book.

Advertisements: about runaways, 46, 48; for slave apprentices, 45

Africans. *See* Slave imports; Slave trade

Age distribution, slave, 56–57, 59; aggregate, 56–57; urban children, 60; urban females, 59–60; and sex ratios, 64

Agriculture: comparative advantage of South in, 7; efficiency of slave labor in, 125; problem of free labor in, 126; slave work compared to city, 63

American Federation of Labor (AFL), agents in South, 131

Anderson, Joseph R., 30, 142 n.5

Apprentices, slave, advertisements for, 45

Artisans: black, decline of, 131; white, petitions of, 29. *See also* Skills; Tradesmen

Badge fees, slave: in cities, 38; in Charleston, 134; in Charleston and Savannah, 108; in Savannah, 137

Badges, use of for hired slaves, 38

Baltimore: commerce, 13; immigrants, 16; large demand elasticity, 122; population data, slave, 52–54; slaveholdings, 19–20; wealth distribution, 13

Becker, Gary: on discrimination, 152 n.4; on skills, 145 n.40

Biases in model, from exclusion of certain variables, 90–91, 94, 99–100

Blacks, free. *See* Free blacks

Blassingame, John, on slave ordinances, 141 n.6

Board money, payment to slaves, 34, 41

Border State cities: commerce, 13; common characteristics, 113–14; immigrant labor, 123; industrial slavery, 27; large demand elasticity, 113, 122; runaways, 108; slave demand, 111; slave demand elasticity, 93. *See also* Baltimore; Louisville; Saint Louis; Washington, D.C.

Bosher, James (Richmond), 21, 45

Brutality, of whites to slaves, 30

Butchers, petitions of white, 29

Cairnes, John Elliott, on decline of urban slavery, 2, 4, 5–6, 7

Camden (S.C.), 31

Central Railroad and Banking Company, 19

Charleston: badge fees, 38, 108; black occupations, 129–30; commerce, 13; 1848 Census, 14–16, 43, 44, 140 n.2; hiring by self-hired slaves, 39; housing, segregation, 40; housing, slave, 40–41; the "Neck," 16 n, 44n, 48; occupations, slave, 42–44; occupations, white males, 13–16; ordinances, slave, 133–34; slave use, decline in, 22, 114; tradesmen petitions, 29; Vesey Conspiracy, 33; wage minima, slave, 30

Charleston, housing differences among wards, 40